ALINA COBB

GLUCOSE GODDESS

COOKBOOK FOR SENIORS

100+

Diabetes & Kidney-Friendly Meals for Balancing Your Blood Sugar

28-DAY MEAL PLAN

for Cutting **Cravings**, Restoring **Energy**, and Feeling Amazing

Disclaimer

Before diving into the "Glucose Goddess Cookbook for Seniors" I want to take a moment to acknowledge something important. The information and recipes in this book are based on my personal journey with the Glucose Goddess Method and the valuable lessons I've learned from Jessie Inchauspé's teachings. However, this book is intended for educational purposes and should not replace professional medical advice or treatment.

If you have any questions about your health, always consult your doctor or a qualified healthcare provider. Everyone's body is different, and what works for one person might not work for another. I've shared recipes and tips that worked for me, but I encourage you to make decisions that best suit your own health needs.

While I've done my best to ensure the accuracy and quality of the content, the recipes and advice in this book are simply guidelines. They're meant to help you reduce inflammation and promote well-being, but results can vary from person to person. If you have any existing health conditions, food allergies, or dietary restrictions, it's essential to talk to a healthcare professional or nutritionist before making any significant changes to your diet or lifestyle.

Your health is your responsibility. By using this book, you agree that you're making informed choices and understand that the content here is not a replacement for professional advice. Listen to your body, and don't hesitate to reach out to your doctor with any concerns or questions about your health or diet.

We disclaim any liability for any loss, injury, or damage incurred as a result of the use or misuse of the information provided in this book. Readers are encouraged to use their own judgment and discretion when applying the content to their personal dietary and health practices.

By using this book, you agree that you are responsible for your own health decisions and understand that the information provided is not a substitute for professional medical advice or treatment. Always seek the advice of a qualified healthcare provider with any questions or concerns you may have regarding your health or dietary needs.

I'm excited for you to join me on this journey, but remember, your well-being is always the top priority!

CONTENTS

Introduction

I'm so glad you're here. This book is more than just a collection of recipes—it's a guide to improving your health, inspired by my personal journey with my parents. Like many families, we've faced health challenges, especially as my parents got older. They struggled with managing their blood sugar, and we were always searching for practical, easy ways to help them feel better and live healthier lives. That's when I discovered the Glucose Goddess Method, created by Jessie Inchauspé. Her teachings changed everything for us.

As I started learning about glucose and how it affects our bodies, I realized that stable blood sugar isn't just about managing diabetes—it's about overall well-being. Glucose spikes, which happen when we eat too many sugary or starchy foods, can make us feel sluggish, hungry all the time, and even affect our mood. But with the right strategies, we can prevent those spikes and enjoy steady energy throughout the day. And the best part? You don't have to give up delicious food to do it!

Why I Wrote This Book

After reading Jessie Inchauspé's books, Glucose Revolution and The Glucose Goddess Method, I started implementing her tips with my parents. Simple things like starting the day with a savory breakfast rich in protein and fiber, eating vegetables first during meals, and avoiding too much sugar at once helped stabilize their blood sugar. I saw the positive changes in their energy levels, mood, and overall health. They felt better, looked better, and had more energy to enjoy life.

It was such a relief to find something that worked—something practical and easy to follow. I wanted to share these simple, life-changing tips with others, especially seniors like my parents, who need extra support in managing their blood sugar and kidney health. That's how this book came to life.

The Power of the Glucose Goddess Method

The Glucose Goddess Method teaches us that managing blood sugar doesn't have to be complicated. By making small changes to how and what we eat, we can see big improvements in how we feel. The method is based on balancing our meals with proteins, healthy fats, and fiber while being mindful of how much sugar and starch we consume. This book offers over 100 easy, diabetes- and kidney-friendly recipes that follow these principles, along with a 28-day meal plan to get you started.

When I started looking for cookbooks that followed the Glucose Goddess Method, I noticed a gap. There weren't many resources that catered to specific dietary needs, like vegetarian, vegan, or gluten-free diets. This was a challenge because my parents needed recipes that worked for their health needs but also fit into their preferences and lifestyle. That's why I made sure this book includes options for everyone, whether you eat meat, follow a plant-based diet, or need gluten-free recipes.

I also wanted to create a book that's not just a cookbook, but a full guide to implementing the Glucose Goddess hacks into your life. In addition to delicious recipes, you'll find helpful tips for meal planning, shopping, and progress tracking so you can stay on track and feel empowered on your health journey.

What You'll Find in This Book

This book will guide you through easy-to-make meals that support balanced blood sugar and good kidney health. The recipes focus on whole, nourishing foods that are both satisfying and beneficial for your body. You'll learn how to incorporate more protein, fiber, and healthy fats into your meals and reduce the foods that cause glucose spikes, like processed sugars and refined carbs.

This book includes.
- **Over 100 recipes** for every meal of the day, plus snacks and desserts
- Options for various dietary needs, including gluten-free, vegetarian, and vegan recipes
- **A 28-day meal plan** to help you get started with balanced eating
- Tips for managing blood sugar and supporting kidney health, especially for seniors

How to Use This Book

The recipes in this book are designed to be simple, flavorful, and easy to prepare. You don't need to be a master chef to enjoy these meals. Most recipes use just a few ingredients, and many can be made in 30 minutes or less. Whether you're cooking for yourself or a loved one, you'll find that these dishes fit seamlessly into your everyday routine.

The 28-day meal plan is a great place to start if you're new to this way of eating. It will help you build healthy habits by showing you exactly what to eat for breakfast, lunch, dinner, and snacks each day. Over time, you'll get a feel for which foods work best for your body, and you can start creating your own balanced meals.

Why This Matters

The Glucose Goddess Method is about more than just managing blood sugar—it's about improving your quality of life. By learning how to balance your meals and prevent glucose spikes, you can enjoy more energy, better mood, and a healthier body. My parents are living proof that these changes work. They've experienced fewer energy crashes, better digestion, and even a reduction in their sugar cravings. Most importantly, they feel empowered to take control of their health.

I hope this book helps you or your loved ones in the same way it's helped my family. The journey to better health doesn't have to be overwhelming. With the right tools, small steps can lead to big changes. Thank you for allowing me to be a part of your health journey. I can't wait to see the positive impact this book will have on your life.

Here's to a healthier, happier you—one meal at a time!

Chapter One

Glucose Goddess Breakfast

Quinoa Breakfast Bowl with Berries

A nutrient-rich breakfast bowl featuring high-fiber quinoa, fresh berries, and chia seeds for steady energy and digestive support.

Ingredients

- 1/2 cup quinoa (uncooked)
- 1 cup unsweetened almond milk
- 1/4 cup fresh mixed berries (blueberries, strawberries)
- 1 tbsp chia seeds
- 1 tsp cinnamon
- 1 tsp honey (optional)

Direction

1. Rinse quinoa under cold water.
2. In a small pot, add quinoa and almond milk. Bring to a boil, then reduce heat and simmer for 15 minutes or until liquid is absorbed.
3. Top with fresh berries, chia seeds, and cinnamon. Drizzle with honey, if desired.

Nutritional Content (per serving):

- Calories: 220
- Total Fat: 5g
- Protein: 6g
- Carbohydrates: 35g
- Sugars: 8g
- Fiber: 7g
- Sodium: 80mg

Cooking Details

- Prep 5 (Mins)
- Time 15 (Mins)
- Serves 2

Spinach and Mushroom Egg Muffins

Easy, portable egg muffins filled with spinach, mushrooms, and cheese, perfect for a protein-packed breakfast on the go.

Ingredients

- 6 large eggs
- 1/2 cup spinach (chopped)
- 1/2 cup mushrooms (diced)
- 1/4 cup shredded low-fat cheese
- 1/4 tsp black pepper
- 1/4 tsp salt
- Olive oil spray

Direction

1. Preheat the oven to 350°F (175°C). Lightly grease a muffin tin with olive oil spray.
2. In a bowl, whisk the eggs with salt and pepper.
3. Add chopped spinach, mushrooms, and cheese to the egg mixture.
4. Pour the mixture evenly into the muffin cups.
5. Bake for 18-20 minutes or until the eggs are set. Let cool before removing from the tin.

Nutritional Content (per serving):

- Calories: 120
- Total Fat: 7g
- Protein: 10g
- Carbohydrates: 3g
- Sugars: 1g
- Fiber: 1g
- Sodium: 180mg

Cooking Details

- Prep 10 (Mins)
- Time 20 (Mins)
- Serves 1

Grilled Lemon Herb Chicken with Quinoa Salad

A refreshing grilled chicken dish paired with a nutrient-dense quinoa salad, perfect for a balanced, protein-rich meal.

Ingredients

- 4 skinless, boneless chicken breasts
- 1 cup quinoa, cooked
- 2 tbsp olive oil; 2 tbsp lemon juice
- 1 tsp dried oregano
- 1 clove garlic, minced
- 1 cucumber, chopped
- 1 cup cherry tomatoes, halved
- ¼ cup feta cheese, crumbled
- Salt and pepper to taste

Direction

1. Preheat the grill to medium-high heat.
2. In a small bowl, mix olive oil, lemon juice, oregano, garlic, salt, and pepper. Marinate chicken breasts for 10 minutes.
3. Grill the chicken for 6-7 minutes per side or until fully cooked.
4. In a large bowl, combine cooked quinoa, cucumber, cherry tomatoes, and feta.
5. Serve grilled chicken over the quinoa salad.

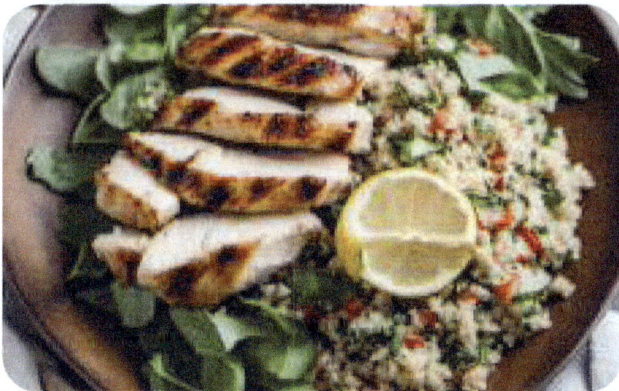

Nutritional Content (per serving):

- Calories: 320
- Total Fat: 12g
- Protein: 32g
- Carbohydrates: 24g
- Sugars: 3g
- Fiber: 4g
- Sodium: 310mg

Cooking Details

Prep 15 (Mins)

Time 20 (Mins)

Serves 4

Sweet Potato Veggie Breakfast Hash

This nutrient-dense breakfast hash made with sweet potatoes and veggies provides a savory and satisfying start to the day.

Ingredients

- 1 medium sweet potato (diced)
- 1/2 cup bell peppers (diced)
- 1/2 cup onions (chopped)
- 2 large eggs
- 1 tbsp olive oil
- 1/4 tsp paprika
- 1/4 tsp black pepper
- 1/4 tsp salt

Direction

1. Heat olive oil in a skillet over medium heat. Add diced sweet potatoes and cook for 10 minutes, stirring occasionally.
2. Add bell peppers, onions, paprika, salt, and pepper. Cook for another 5-7 minutes until tender.
3. In a separate pan, fry or poach eggs to your liking.
4. Serve the hash topped with eggs.

Nutritional Content (per serving):

- Calories: 280
- Total Fat: 18g
- Protein: 11g
- Carbohydrates: 24g
- Sugars: 1g
- Fiber: 7g
- Sodium: 200mg

Cooking Details

Prep 10 (Mins)

Time 5 (Mins)

Serves 1

Chia Seed Pudding with Coconut Milk

A fiber-rich, make-ahead breakfast that combines whole grains and healthy fats, perfect for maintaining steady glucose levels.

Ingredients

- 1/4 cup chia seeds
- 1 cup unsweetened coconut milk
- 1 tsp vanilla extract
- 1 tsp honey or maple syrup (optional)
- Fresh berries for topping

Direction

- Mix chia seeds, coconut milk, vanilla extract, and honey in a jar or bowl.
- Stir well and let sit for 5 minutes, then stir again to prevent clumping.
- Cover and refrigerate overnight.
- In the morning, stir the pudding and top with fresh berries.

Nutritional Content (per serving):

- Calories: 190
- Total Fat: 12g
- Protein: 4g
- Carbohydrates: 15g
- Sugars: 4g
- Fiber: 9g
- Sodium: 40mg

Cooking Details

- Prep 5 (Mins)
- Time 0 (Mins)
- Serves 2

Turkey and Veggie Stir-Fry

A quick, protein-packed turkey stir-fry loaded with colorful veggies, perfect for a quick, nutritious breakfast.

Ingredients

- 1 lb ground turkey
- 2 tbsp olive oil; 1 red bell pepper, sliced
- 1 zucchini, sliced
- 1 cup broccoli florets
- 1 tbsp low-sodium soy sauce
- 1 tsp ginger, grated; 1 tbsp olive oil
- 1 clove garlic, minced
- 2 tbsp sesame seeds
- 2 tbsp fresh cilantro, chopped

Direction

1. Heat olive oil in a large skillet over medium heat.
2. Add ground turkey and cook until browned, about 5-6 minutes.
3. Add bell pepper, zucchini, broccoli, ginger, and garlic. Stir-fry for 5-6 minutes until veggies are tender.
4. Stir in soy sauce and sesame seeds.
5. Garnish with fresh cilantro before serving.

Nutritional Content (per serving):

- Calories: 290
- Total Fat: 14g
- Protein: 26g
- Carbohydrates: 12g
- Sugars: 4g
- Fiber: 3g
- Sodium: 280mg

Cooking Details

- Prep 10 (Mins)
- Time 25 (Mins)
- Serves 4

Chickpea Flour Pancakes

A high-protein, low-carb pancake alternative using chickpea flour, which provides steady energy and supports blood sugar regulation.

Ingredients

- 1 cup chickpea flour
- 1/2 cup water
- 1/4 tsp turmeric
- 1/4 tsp black pepper
- 1 tbsp olive oil (for cooking)
- Fresh cilantro (for garnish)

Direction

- In a bowl, whisk chickpea flour, water, turmeric, and black pepper until smooth.
- Heat olive oil in a non-stick skillet over medium heat.
- Pour 1/4 cup of batter into the skillet and cook for 2-3 minutes on each side until golden brown.
- Garnish with fresh cilantro before serving.

Nutritional Content (per serving):

- Calories: 200
- Total Fat: 6g
- Protein: 9g
- Carbohydrates: 26g
- Sugars: 1g
- Fiber: 6g
- Sodium: 180mg

Cooking Details

- Prep 10 (Mins)
- Time 10 (Mins)
- Serves 2

Greek Yogurt Parfait with Walnuts and Strawberries

A creamy, high-protein yogurt parfait with crunchy walnuts and fresh strawberries, offering a well-balanced, low-sugar breakfast.

Ingredients

- 1/2 cup plain Greek yogurt
- 1/4 cup strawberries (sliced)
- 1 tbsp chopped walnuts
- 1 tsp chia seeds
- 1 tsp honey or stevia (optional)

Direction

1. Layer Greek yogurt with strawberries, chopped walnuts, and chia seeds in a bowl or glass.
2. Drizzle with honey or stevia if desired, and serve.

Nutritional Content (per serving):

- Calories: 200
- Total Fat: 10g
- Protein: 14g
- Carbohydrates: 16g
- Sugars: 6g
- Fiber: 3g
- Sodium: 50mg

Cooking Details

- Prep 5 (Mins)
- Time 0 (Mins)
- Serves 1

Cottage Cheese and Cucumber Toast

A light, refreshing breakfast combining the protein of cottage cheese with hydrating cucumbers on whole grain toast.

Ingredients

- 1 slice whole grain bread (toasted)
- 1/3 cup low-fat cottage cheese
- 1/4 cucumber (sliced)
- 1/4 tsp black pepper
- 1/4 tsp lemon juice
- Fresh dill (for garnish).

Direction

- Spread cottage cheese on the toasted whole grain bread.
- Top with cucumber slices, black pepper, and lemon juice.
- Garnish with fresh dill before serving.

Nutritional Content
(per serving):

- Calories: 170
- Total Fat: 3g
- Protein: 11g
- Carbohydrates: 24g
- Sugars: 4g
- Fiber: 4g
- Sodium: 280mg

Cooking Details

Prep   5   (Mins)

Time   0   (Mins)

Serves   1

Almond Flour Waffles

These waffles made with almond flour are low in carbohydrates and provide a delicious gluten-free, diabetes-friendly breakfast option.

Ingredients

- 1 cup almond flour
- 2 large eggs
- 1/4 cup unsweetened almond milk
- 1/2 tsp baking powder
- 1/2 tsp vanilla extract
- 1 tsp honey or stevia (optional)

Direction

1. Preheat the waffle iron.
2. In a bowl, whisk together almond flour, eggs, almond milk, baking powder, and vanilla extract until smooth.
3. Pour the batter into the waffle iron and cook according to the manufacturer's instructions until golden brown.
4. Serve with a drizzle of honey or stevia if desired.

Nutritional Content
(per serving):

- Calories: 290
- Total Fat: 22g
- Protein: 12g
- Carbohydrates: 10g
- Sugars: 3g
- Fiber: 4g
- Sodium: 180mg

Cooking Details

Prep   5   (Mins)

Time   10   (Mins)

Serves   2

Chapter Two

Glucose Goddess Lunch

Turkey & Avocado Wrap with Spinach

A simple, low-carb, high-protein wrap that's perfect for a quick lunch

Ingredients

- 4 slices of turkey breast (low sodium)
- 1/2 avocado, sliced
- 2 large whole-grain or low-carb wraps
- 1 cup fresh spinach
- 1 tbsp Dijon mustard
- 1 tbsp plain Greek yogurt

Direction

- Spread Dijon mustard and Greek yogurt evenly over each wrap.
- Layer the turkey, spinach, and avocado slices onto the wraps.
- Roll up the wraps tightly and slice them in half.
- Serve with a side salad or a few vegetable sticks like cucumbers or carrots.

Nutritional Content (per serving):	Cooking Details
Calories: 350 kcal	Prep 10 (Mins)
Total Fat: 16g	Time 0 (Mins)
Protein: 24g	
Carbohydrates: 27g	
Sugars: 2g	Serves 2
Fiber: 7g	
Sodium: 420mg	

Zucchini Noodles with Pesto and Grilled Chicken

A low-carb pasta alternative using zucchini noodles, paired with grilled chicken for lean protein and a flavorful homemade pesto.

Ingredients

- 2 medium zucchini, spiralized
- 2 chicken breasts, grilled and sliced
- 1/4 cup fresh basil leaves
- 1/4 cup olive oil
- 1/4 cup pine nuts or walnuts
- 1/4 cup grated Parmesan cheese
- 1 garlic clove
- Salt and pepper to taste.

Direction

1. Grill or pan-sear the chicken breasts for 6-7 minutes per side until fully cooked. Set aside.
2. In a blender or food processor, combine basil, olive oil, pine nuts, Parmesan, garlic, salt, and pepper to make the pesto.
3. Toss the zucchini noodles in the pesto until well coated.
4. Serve the zucchini noodles with sliced grilled chicken on top.

Nutritional Content (per serving):	Cooking Details
Calories: 320 kcal	Prep 15 (Mins)
Total Fat: 24g	Time 15 (Mins)
Protein: 23g	
Carbohydrates: 8g	
Sugars: 4g	Serves 4
Fiber: 3g	
Sodium: 200mg	

Egg Salad on Whole Grain Toast

A classic egg salad served on whole grain toast, rich in protein and fiber, making it a satisfying and nutritious lunch.

Ingredients

- 6 hard-boiled eggs, chopped
- 1/4 cup Greek yogurt (or mayo)
- 1 tsp mustard
- 1/4 cup celery, chopped
- Salt and pepper to taste
- 4 slices whole grain bread

Direction

- In a bowl, mix chopped eggs, Greek yogurt, mustard, celery, salt, and pepper until well combined.
- Toast whole grain bread slices.
- Spoon egg salad over the toasted bread and serve.

Nutritional Content (per serving):

- Calories: 220 kcal
- Total Fat: 8g
- Protein: 14g
- Carbohydrates: 26g
- Sugars: 2g
- Fiber: 4g
- Sodium: 310mg

Cooking Details

- Prep 10 (Mins)
- Time 10 (Mins)
- Serves 4

Roasted Vegetable and Hummus Bowl

A colorful bowl filled with roasted vegetables and creamy hummus, packed with nutrients and fiber for a balanced lunch.

Ingredients

- 2 cups assorted vegetables (bell peppers, zucchini, carrots)
- 1 cup cooked quinoa
- 1/2 cup hummus
- 2 tbsp olive oil
- Salt and pepper to taste.

Direction

1. Preheat the oven to 425°F (220°C). Toss vegetables with olive oil, salt, and pepper. Spread on a baking sheet.
2. Roast for 20-25 minutes until tender and slightly caramelized.
3. In a bowl, layer cooked quinoa, roasted vegetables, and top with hummus.

Nutritional Content (per serving):

- Calories: 300 kcal
- Total Fat: 14g
- Protein: 10g
- Carbohydrates: 40g
- Sugars: 5g
- Fiber: 8g
- Sodium: 200mg

Cooking Details

- Prep 15 (Mins)
- Time 25 (Mins)
- Serves 4

Baked Tilapia with Lemon and Herbs

Baked tilapia seasoned with lemon and herbs, offering a light and flavorful protein source. This dish pairs well with steamed vegetables for a complete meal.

Ingredients

- 4 tilapia fillets
- 2 tbsp olive oil
- 2 tbsp lemon juice
- 1 tsp dried oregano
- Salt and pepper to taste
- Lemon slices for garnish.

Direction

- Preheat the oven to 375°F (190°C). Place tilapia fillets on a baking sheet lined with parchment paper.
- Drizzle olive oil and lemon juice over the fillets, and season with oregano, salt, and pepper.
- Bake for 12-15 minutes until the fish is opaque and flakes easily with a fork.
- Garnish with lemon slices before serving.

Nutritional Content (per serving):

- Calories: 220 kcal
- Total Fat: 10g
- Protein: 25g
- Carbohydrates: 2g
- Sugars: 0g
- Fiber: 0g
- Sodium: 90mg

Cooking Details

- Prep 15 (Mins)
- Time 25 (Mins)
- Serves 4

Quinoa Salad with Chickpeas and Spinach

A hearty quinoa salad packed with protein-rich chickpeas and fresh spinach, this dish is filling and nutritious, ideal for a healthy lunch.

Ingredients

- 1 cup quinoa, cooked
- 1 can chickpeas, drained and rinsed
- 2 cups fresh spinach, chopped
- 1/4 cup red onion, diced
- 1/4 cup feta cheese, crumbled (optional)
- 2 tbsp olive oil
- 2 tbsp lemon juice
- Salt and pepper to taste

Direction

1. In a large bowl, combine cooked quinoa, chickpeas, spinach, red onion, and feta cheese.
2. In a small bowl, whisk together olive oil, lemon juice, salt, and pepper.
3. Pour the dressing over the salad and toss to combine.

Nutritional Content (per serving):

- Calories: 280 kcal
- Total Fat: 12g
- Protein: 10g
- Carbohydrates: 36g
- Sugars: 3g
- Fiber: 8g
- Sodium: 320mg

Cooking Details

- Prep 10 (Mins)
- Time 15 (Mins)
- Serves 4

Chapter Three

Glucose Goddess Dinner

Grilled Lemon Garlic Chicken with Steamed Broccoli

This simple grilled chicken dish, seasoned with lemon and garlic, is paired with fiber-rich steamed broccoli, making it a wholesome & balanced meal.

Ingredients

- 4 chicken breasts
- 2 tbsp olive oil
- 2 cloves garlic, minced
- 1 lemon, juiced
- Salt and pepper to taste
- 1 large head of broccoli, cut into florets.

Direction

- Preheat the grill to medium heat.
- In a bowl, mix olive oil, garlic, lemon juice, salt, and pepper. Marinate chicken in this mixture for 10 minutes.
- Grill chicken for 6-8 minutes on each side, or until fully cooked.
- Steam broccoli for 5-7 minutes, until tender.
- Serve chicken with steamed broccoli on the side.

Nutritional Content (per serving):	Cooking Details
- Calories: 320 kcal - Total Fat: 14g - Protein: 40g - Carbohydrates: 6g - Sugars: 2g - Fiber: 3g - Sodium: 250mg	Prep 10 (Mins) Time 20 (Mins) Serves 4

Quinoa-Stuffed Bell Peppers

Quinoa-stuffed bell peppers offer a fiber-rich, nutritious, and diabetic-friendly meal that helps maintain balanced blood sugar levels.

Ingredients

- 4 large bell peppers
- 1 cup quinoa, cooked
- 1/2 cup black beans, drained and rinsed
- 1/2 cup corn kernels (fresh or frozen)
- 1/2 cup diced tomatoes
- 2 tbsp olive oil
- 1 tsp cumin
- Salt and pepper to taste

Direction

1. Preheat the oven to 375°F (190°C).
2. Cut the tops off the bell peppers and remove seeds.
3. In a bowl, mix quinoa, black beans, corn, tomatoes, olive oil, cumin, salt, and pepper.
4. Stuff the bell peppers with the quinoa mixture and place in a baking dish.
5. Bake for 20-25 minutes until the peppers are tender.

Nutritional Content (per serving):	Cooking Details
- Calories: 290 kcal - Total Fat: 10g - Protein: 8g - Carbohydrates: 40g - Sugars: 8g - Fiber: 8g - Sodium: 300mg	Prep 15 (Mins) Time 25 (Mins) Serves 4

Baked Cod with Spinach and Tomatoes

Cod baked with spinach and tomatoes is a nutritious, low-calorie meal packed with lean protein and antioxidants.

Ingredients

- 4 cod fillets
- 2 cups spinach, chopped
- 1 cup cherry tomatoes, halved
- 1 tbsp olive oil
- 2 cloves garlic, minced
- Salt and pepper to taste

Direction

- Preheat the oven to 400°F (200°C).
- In a baking dish, place spinach and tomatoes, and drizzle with olive oil.
- Lay cod fillets on top and sprinkle with garlic, salt, and pepper.
- Bake for 15-20 minutes, until the fish flakes easily with a fork.

Nutritional Content (per serving):

- Calories: 240 kcal
- Total Fat: 8g
- Protein: 32g
- Carbohydrates: 6g
- Sugars: 3g
- Fiber: 2g
- Sodium: 170mg

Cooking Details

- Prep 10 (Mins)
- Time 20 (Mins)
- Serves 4

Turkey and Zucchini Skillet

Ground turkey and zucchini are cooked together in this low-carb dish that offers plenty of protein and fiber while being light and easy to digest.

Ingredients

- 1 lb ground turkey
- 2 medium zucchinis, sliced
- 1 onion, diced
- 1 tbsp olive oil
- 1 tsp dried oregano
- Salt and pepper to taste

Direction

1. Heat olive oil in a large skillet over medium heat.
2. Add onion and cook until softened, about 5 minutes.
3. Add ground turkey and cook until browned.
4. Stir in zucchini, oregano, salt, and pepper, and cook for an additional 5 minutes until zucchini is tender.

Nutritional Content (per serving):

- Calories: 260 kcal
- Total Fat: 12g
- Protein: 25g
- Carbohydrates: 8g
- Sugars: 4g
- Fiber: 3g
- Sodium: 200mg

Cooking Details

- Prep 10 (Mins)
- Time 15 (Mins)
- Serves 4

Chicken and Cauliflower Rice Stir-Fry

This stir-fry replaces regular rice with cauliflower rice, making it a low-carb, diabetic-friendly alternative packed with veggies and lean protein.

Ingredients

- 2 chicken breasts, cubed
- 4 cups cauliflower rice (store-bought or homemade)
- 1 cup bell peppers, sliced
- 1 carrot, sliced
- 2 tbsp soy sauce (low sodium)
- 1 tbsp sesame oil
- 2 cloves garlic, minced
- Salt and pepper to taste

Direction

- Heat sesame oil in a large skillet over medium heat.
- Add garlic and cook for 1 minute. Add chicken and stir-fry until cooked through, about 5-7 minutes.
- Add bell peppers, carrots, and cauliflower rice. Stir in soy sauce and cook for an additional 5 minutes until vegetables are tender.
- Season with salt and pepper to taste.

Nutritional Content (per serving):

- Calories: 230 kcal
- Total Fat: 9g
- Protein: 28g
- Carbohydrates: 10g
- Sugars: 5g
- Fiber: 4g
- Sodium: 300mg

Cooking Details

- Prep: 15 (Mins)
- Time: 15 (Mins)
- Serves: 4

Lentil Soup with Spinach

A warm, hearty lentil soup rich in fiber and plant-based protein, ideal for a cozy and healthy dinner.

Ingredients

- 1 cup dried lentils
- 4 cups vegetable broth (low sodium)
- 2 cups spinach, chopped
- 1 carrot, diced
- 1 onion, diced
- 2 cloves garlic, minced
- 1 tbsp olive oil
- 1 tsp cumin
- Salt and pepper to taste.

Direction

1. Heat olive oil in a large pot over medium heat.
2. Add onion, carrot, and garlic, and cook until softened, about 5 minutes.
3. Stir in lentils, vegetable broth, and cumin. Bring to a boil, then simmer for 25-30 minutes until lentils are tender.
4. Stir in spinach and cook for an additional 2 minutes. Season with salt and pepper to taste.

Nutritional Content (per serving):

- Calories: 250 kcal
- Total Fat: 6g
- Protein: 15g
- Carbohydrates: 35g
- Sugars: 4g
- Fiber: 12g
- Sodium: 350mg

Cooking Details

- Prep: 10 (Mins)
- Time: 30 (Mins)
- Serves: 4

Lemon Garlic Baked Tilapia

This baked tilapia dish is flavorful, light, and high in lean protein, making it a perfect dinner for blood sugar balance.

Ingredients

- 4 tilapia fillets
- 1 lemon, juiced and zested
- 2 tbsp olive oil
- 2 cloves garlic, minced
- Salt and pepper to taste
- Fresh parsley for garnish

Direction

- Preheat the oven to 400°F (200°C).
- In a bowl, mix olive oil, lemon juice, zest, garlic, salt, and pepper.
- Place tilapia fillets in a baking dish and pour the mixture over the fish.
- Bake for 12-15 minutes until the fish flakes easily with a fork.
- Garnish with fresh parsley and serve.

Nutritional Content (per serving):

- Calories: 220 kcal
- Total Fat: 12g
- Protein: 28g
- Carbohydrates: 2g
- Sugars: 0g
- Fiber: 0g
- Sodium: 180mg

Cooking Details

- Prep 5 (Mins)
- Time 15 (Mins)
- Serves 4

Chicken and Sweet Potato Bake

Chicken breast and sweet potatoes come together in this balanced meal rich in fiber, vitamins, and lean protein.

Ingredients

- 4 chicken breasts
- 2 medium sweet potatoes, diced
- 1 onion, sliced
- 2 tbsp olive oil
- 1 tsp paprika
- 1 tsp garlic powder
- Salt and pepper to taste

Direction

1. Preheat the oven to 375°F (190°C).
2. In a bowl, mix almond flour and parmesan cheese. Dip eggplant slices in beaten egg, then coat with almond flour mixture.
3. Lay the eggplant on a baking sheet and drizzle with olive oil. Bake for 20 minutes, flipping halfway.
4. Remove from the oven and top each slice with marinara sauce and mozzarella. Bake for another 10 minutes, until cheese is melted and bubbly.

Nutritional Content (per serving):

- Calories: 380 kcal
- Total Fat: 12g
- Protein: 38g
- Carbohydrates: 30g
- Sugars: 8g
- Fiber: 5g
- Sodium: 300mg

Cooking Details

- Prep 10 (Mins)
- Time 40 (Mins)
- Serves 4

Zucchini Noodles with Pesto and Grilled Chicken

A low-carb twist on pasta, zucchini noodles with pesto and grilled chicken provide a flavorful and nutrient-dense meal.

Ingredients

- 4 zucchinis, spiralized
- 2 chicken breasts, grilled and sliced
- 1/4 cup basil pesto (store-bought or homemade)
- 2 tbsp olive oil
- Salt and pepper to taste

Direction

- Spiralize the zucchinis to make noodles.
- Heat olive oil in a pan and sauté zucchini noodles for 3-4 minutes until tender.
- Toss the zucchini noodles with pesto and grilled chicken slices.
- Serve warm with a sprinkle of salt and pepper.

Nutritional Content (per serving):

- Calories: 300 kcal
- Total Fat: 18g
- Protein: 30g
- Carbohydrates: 10g
- Sugars: 5g
- Fiber: 4g
- Sodium: 220mg

Cooking Details

- Prep 10 (Mins)
- Time 35 (Mins)
- Serves 4

Grilled Turkey Burgers with Avocado

These grilled turkey burgers topped with heart-healthy avocado offer a flavorful, low-carb alternative to traditional burgers.

Ingredients

- 1 lb ground turkey
- 1 avocado, sliced
- 1 tbsp olive oil
- 1 tsp garlic powder
- Salt and pepper to taste
- 4 lettuce leaves (for wrapping)

Direction

1. Preheat grill to medium heat.
2. In a bowl, mix ground turkey, garlic powder, salt, and pepper. Form into 4 patties.
3. Grill the patties for 5 minutes on each side, or until fully cooked.
4. Serve burgers wrapped in lettuce leaves, topped with avocado slices.

Nutritional Content (per serving):

- Calories: 300 kcal
- Total Fat: 20g
- Protein: 25g
- Carbohydrates: 6g
- Sugars: 1g
- Fiber: 4g
- Sodium: 180mg

Cooking Details

- Prep 10 (Mins)
- Time 10 (Mins)
- Serves 4

Sautéed Shrimp with Garlic and Spinach

A quick and light dinner of shrimp sautéed with garlic and spinach, providing a high-protein, low-carb meal.

Ingredients

- 1 lb shrimp, peeled and deveined
- 4 cups spinach
- 2 tbsp olive oil
- 3 cloves garlic, minced
- 1/4 tsp red pepper flakes
- 1 tbsp lemon juice
- Salt and pepper to taste

Direction

- Heat olive oil in a large skillet over medium heat. Add garlic and red pepper flakes, and sauté for 1 minute.
- Add shrimp to the skillet and cook for 2-3 minutes on each side until pink and cooked through.
- Stir in spinach and cook until wilted, about 2 minutes.
- Drizzle with lemon juice and season with salt and pepper before serving.

Nutritional Content (per serving):	Cooking Details	
Calories: 220 kcal	Prep	10 (Mins)
Total Fat: 12g		
Protein: 25g	Time	10 (Mins)
Carbohydrates: 4g		
Sugars: 1g		
Fiber: 2g	Serves	4
Sodium: 380mg		

Baked Cod with Lemon and Herbs

A simple, low-carb dinner featuring baked cod seasoned with lemon and fresh herbs for a light, heart-healthy meal.

Ingredients

- 4 cod fillets (about 5 oz each)
- 2 tbsp olive oil
- 2 tbsp lemon juice
- 1 tsp dried oregano
- 1 tsp dried thyme
- Salt and pepper to taste

Direction

1. Preheat oven to 400°F (200°C). Place cod fillets on a baking sheet lined with parchment paper.
2. Drizzle fillets with olive oil and lemon juice. Sprinkle with oregano, thyme, salt, and pepper.
3. Bake for 12-15 minutes, until cod is cooked through and flakes easily with a fork.

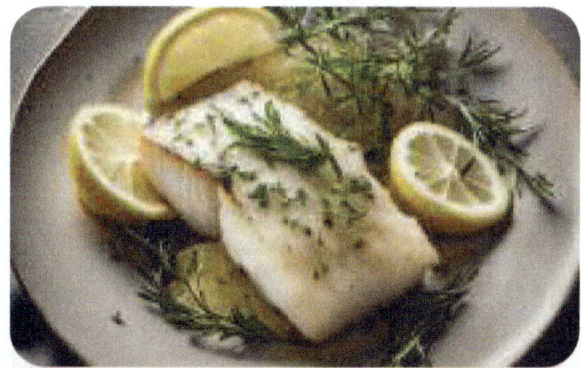

Nutritional Content (per serving):	Cooking Details	
Calories: 230 kcal	Prep	5 (Mins)
Total Fat: 10g		
Protein: 32g	Time	15 (Mins)
Carbohydrates: 2g		
Sugars: 0g		
Fiber: 1g	Serves	4
Sodium: 220mg		

Chapter Four

Glucose Goddess Soup

CREAMY BROCCOLI AND SPINACH SOUP

A fiber-rich, low-calorie soup that combines non starchy broccoli and spinach, perfect for controlling blood sugar while providing essential vitamins and minerals for seniors.

Ingredients
- 2 cups broccoli florets
- 2 cups fresh spinach
- 1 small onion, diced
- 2 cloves garlic, minced
- 4 cups low-sodium vegetable broth
- 1/4 cup unsweetened almond milk
- 1 tbsp olive oil
- Salt and pepper to taste

Direction
1. In a large pot, heat olive oil over medium heat. Sauté onion and garlic for 3-4 minutes until softened.
2. Add broccoli and vegetable broth. Bring to a boil, then reduce heat and simmer for 15 minutes until broccoli is tender.
3. Add spinach and cook for another 2 minutes until wilted.
4. Use an immersion blender to blend the soup until smooth.
5. Stir in almond milk, season with salt and pepper, and serve hot.

Nutritional Content (per serving)	Storage Tips	Cooking and Ingredients Tips
- Calories: 130 kcal - Total Fat: 6g - Protein: 5g - Carbohydrates: 16g - Sugars: 5g - Fiber: 6g - Sodium: 320mg	Store leftovers in an airtight container in the fridge for up to 4 days. Reheat gently on the stove.	- For added creaminess, use a splash of coconut milk or oat milk. - Make sure not to overcook the vegetables to preserve nutrients and texture.

LENTIL AND SPINACH SOUP

Packed with plant-based protein and fiber, this lentil and spinach soup helps stabilize blood sugar levels and support digestion, making it an excellent meal for seniors

Ingredients
- 1 cup dry green or brown lentils
- 4 cups low-sodium vegetable broth
- 2 cups fresh spinach, chopped
- 1 carrot, diced
- 1 celery stalk, diced
- 1 small onion, chopped

Direction
1. Heat olive oil in a pot over medium heat. Add onion, carrot, and celery, sautéing for 5 minutes until softened.
2. Stir in cumin and cook for 1 minute until fragrant.
3. Add lentils, bay leaf, and broth. Bring to a boil, then reduce heat to low and simmer for 20 minutes until lentils are tender.
4. Stir in spinach and cook for another 2 minutes. Remove bay leaf and season with salt and pepper.

Nutritional Content (per serving)	Storage Tips	Cooking and Ingredients Tips
- Calories: 230 kcal - Total Fat: 7g - Protein: 13g - Carbohydrates: 31g - Sugars: 5g - Fiber: 12g - Sodium: 320mg	This soup stores well in the refrigerator for up to 5 days. It also freezes well for up to 3 months.	- Rinse lentils before cooking to remove debris and enhance flavor. - You can substitute kale for spinach for a heartier texture.

CHICKEN AND QUINOA VEGETABLE SOUP

A nutritious, protein-packed soup featuring lean chicken, quinoa, and an array of vegetables for a low-GI, fiber-rich meal.

Cooking Details

Prep 15 (Mins)

Time 25 (Mins)

Serves 4

Ingredients

- 1 chicken breast (about 5 oz), cooked and shredded
- 1/2 cup quinoa, rinsed
- 1 zucchini, diced
- 1 carrot, diced
- 1 onion, chopped
- 3 cups low-sodium chicken broth
- 1 tbsp olive oil   ;   1 tsp thyme

Direction

1. Heat olive oil in a pot over medium heat. Add onion, garlic, carrot, and zucchini, sautéing for 5 minutes until softened.
2. Stir in thyme, quinoa, and chicken broth. Bring to a boil, then reduce heat to low and simmer for 15 minutes until quinoa is cooked.
3. Stir in shredded chicken and cook for another 5 minutes. Season with salt and pepper to taste.

Nutritional Content (per serving)	Storage Tips	Cooking and Ingredients Tips
- Calories: 260 kcal - Total Fat: 8g - Protein: 20g - Carbohydrates: 26g - Sugars: 5g - Fiber: 6g - Sodium: 310mg	Store in an airtight container in the fridge for up to 4 days. The soup can also be frozen for up to 3 months.	- Cook the chicken breast ahead of time to save prep time. - Rinse quinoa thoroughly to remove its natural bitterness.

ROASTED RED PEPPER AND TOMATO SOUP

This vibrant, antioxidant-rich soup combines roasted red peppers and tomatoes for a delicious, low-sodium dish that supports heart and blood sugar health.

Cooking Details

Prep 10 (Mins)

Time 30 (Mins)

Serves 4

Ingredients

- 3 large red bell peppers, roasted and peeled
- 4 large tomatoes, chopped
- 1 small onion, diced
- 2 cloves garlic, minced
- 4 cups low-sodium vegetable broth
- 1 tbsp olive oil ; Salt and pepper to taste
- Fresh basil for garnish

Direction

1. Heat olive oil in a pot over medium heat. Add onion and garlic, sautéing for 5 minutes until soft.
2. Add roasted peppers, tomatoes, and broth. Bring to a boil, then reduce heat to a simmer for 20 minutes.
3. Use an immersion blender or transfer to a blender to puree until smooth.
4. Season with salt and pepper, then serve garnished with fresh basil. Serve with Brown rice.

Nutritional Content (per serving)	Storage Tips	Cooking and Ingredients Tips
- Calories: 150 kcal - Total Fat: 5g - Protein: 3g - Carbohydrates: 24g - Sugars: 12g - Fiber: 6g - Sodium: 280mg	Store in the fridge for up to 4 days, or freeze for up to 3 months. Reheat gently to preserve flavor.	- To roast the peppers, place them under the broiler, turning frequently, until blackened. Peel the skin after cooling. - Add a touch of Greek yogurt for extra creaminess.

CARROT GINGER SOUP

This warming soup combines the natural sweetness of carrots with the anti-inflammatory benefits of ginger, creating a light, diabetic-friendly option.

Cooking Details

🗒 Prep 10 (Mins)

🕐 Time 25 (Mins)

🍴 Serves 4

Ingredients

- 4 large carrots, peeled and chopped
- 1-inch piece fresh ginger, peeled and minced
- 1 small onion, diced
- 2 cloves garlic, minced
- 4 cups low-sodium vegetable broth
- 1 tbsp olive oil
- Salt and pepper to taste
- Fresh cilantro for garnish

Direction

1. Heat olive oil in a large pot over medium heat. Add onion, garlic, and ginger, sautéing for 5 minutes.
2. Add carrots and vegetable broth, and bring to a boil. Lower heat and simmer for 20 minutes until carrots are tender.
3. Puree the soup with an immersion blender or in a blender until smooth. Season with salt and pepper, and garnish with cilantro.

Nutritional Content (per serving)	Storage Tips	Cooking and Ingredients Tips
• Calories: 130 kcal • Total Fat: 4g • Protein: 2g • Carbohydrates: 22g • Sugars: 10g • Fiber: 6g • Sodium: 250mg	This soup can be stored in the fridge for up to 4 days, or frozen for 2-3 months.	• Use fresh ginger for a more robust flavor, and adjust the amount based on your spice preference. • Add a dollop of coconut cream for a creamier texture.

BUTTERNUT SQUASH AND TURMERIC SOUP

With a naturally sweet and nutty flavor, this butternut squash soup is boosted with turmeric, an anti-inflammatory spice, to support joint and heart health.

Cooking Details

🗒 Prep 10 (Mins)

🕐 Time 30 (Mins)

🍴 Serves 4

Ingredients

- 1 medium butternut squash, peeled and cubed
- 1 onion, chopped
- 1-inch piece of fresh turmeric or 1 tsp ground turmeric
- 3 cups low-sodium vegetable broth
- 1 tbsp olive oil   ; 1 tsp ground cumin
- Salt and pepper to taste
- Fresh parsley for garnish

Direction

1. Heat olive oil in a pot over medium heat. Add onion and turmeric, sautéing for 5 minutes.
2. Add cubed squash, cumin, and broth. Bring to a boil, then reduce heat and simmer for 20-25 minutes until squash is tender.
3. Puree the soup using an immersion blender until smooth. Season with salt and pepper.

Nutritional Content (per serving)	Storage Tips	Cooking and Ingredients Tips
• Calories: 150 kcal • Total Fat: 5g • Protein: 3g • Carbohydrates: 24g • Sugars: 12g • Fiber: 6g • Sodium: 280mg	Store in the fridge for up to 5 days or freeze for 3 months.	• Adding a pinch of black pepper enhances the absorption of turmeric's beneficial compounds. • You can also roast the squash beforehand to deepen the flavor.

ZUCCHINI AND BASIL SOUP

This warming soup combines the natural sweetness of carrots with the anti-inflammatory benefits of ginger, creating a light, diabetic-friendly option.

Ingredients

- 4 medium zucchini, chopped
- 1 small onion, diced
- 2 cloves garlic, minced
- 4 cups low-sodium vegetable broth
- 1 tbsp olive oil
- 1/2 cup fresh basil leaves
- Salt and pepper to taste
- 1/4 cup unsweetened almond milk

Direction

1. Heat olive oil in a large pot over medium heat. Add the onion and garlic, sautéing for 5 minutes.
2. Add the zucchini and vegetable broth. Bring to a boil, then reduce heat and simmer for 15 minutes until zucchini is tender.
3. Use an immersion blender or transfer to a blender to puree the soup until smooth.
4. Stir in almond milk and season with salt and pepper. Garnish with fresh basil leaves before serving.

Nutritional Content (per serving)	Storage Tips	Cooking and Ingredients Tips
• Calories: 110 kcal • Total Fat: 5g • Protein: 3g • Carbohydrates: 13g • Sugars: 6g • Fiber: 4g • Sodium: 240mg	Store in an airtight container in the refrigerator for up to 4 days. You can freeze this soup for up to 2 months.	• Add a sprinkle of nutritional yeast for a cheesy flavor without adding dairy. • Basil can be substituted with cilantro for a different flavor profile.

SPLIT PEA AND HAM SOUP

A hearty and filling soup that provides plant-based protein from peas and lean protein from ham, helping to stabilize blood sugar and satisfy hunger.

Ingredients

- 1 cup dry split peas, rinsed
- 1 small onion, diced
- 2 carrots, diced
- 1 celery stalk, diced
- 3 cups low-sodium chicken broth
- 1 cup water
- 4 oz lean ham, diced
- 1 bay leaf ; Salt and pepper to taste

Direction

1. In a large pot, combine split peas, onion, carrots, celery, broth, water, and bay leaf. Bring to a boil, then lower the heat and simmer for 40 minutes.
2. Add diced ham and cook for another 5-10 minutes until the peas are soft and the soup thickens.
3. Remove the bay leaf and season with salt and pepper to taste.

Nutritional Content (per serving)	Storage Tips	Cooking and Ingredients Tips
• Calories: 250 kcal • Total Fat: 4g • Protein: 20g • Carbohydrates: 33g • Sugars: 5g • Fiber: 12g • Sodium: 320mg	This soup can be refrigerated for up to 5 days. Freeze individual portions for easy meals for up to 3 months.	• For a vegetarian option, omit the ham and use vegetable broth. • If the soup becomes too thick, add water or broth to achieve your desired consistency.

MUSHROOM BARLEY SOUP

This warming soup combines the natural sweetness of carrots with the anti-inflammatory benefits of ginger, creating a light, diabetic-friendly option.

Ingredients

- 1/2 cup pearl barley, rinsed
- 2 cups mushrooms, sliced
- 1 small onion, chopped
- 2 cloves garlic, minced
- 4 cups low-sodium vegetable broth
- 1 tbsp olive oil
- 1 tsp thyme
- Salt and pepper to taste

Direction

1. Heat olive oil in a large pot over medium heat. Add onions, garlic, and mushrooms, sautéing for 5-6 minutes until softened.
2. Add thyme, barley, and broth. Bring to a boil, then reduce heat and simmer for 30 minutes until barley is tender.
3. Season with salt and pepper to taste before serving.

Nutritional Content (per serving)	Storage Tips	Cooking and Ingredients Tips
<ul><li>Calories: 210 kcal</li><li>Total Fat: 6g</li><li>Protein: 6g</li><li>Carbohydrates: 36g</li><li>Sugars: 4g</li><li>Fiber: 8g</li><li>Sodium: 260mg</li></ul>	Store in the fridge for up to 5 days, or freeze for up to 3 months. Reheat gently on the stove.	<ul><li>For a creamier version, add a splash of unsweetened almond milk or coconut milk.</li><li>You can substitute quinoa for barley to reduce cooking time.</li></ul>

THAI COCONUT CHICKEN SOUP (TOM KHA GAI)

This flavorful, diabetic-friendly Thai soup combines the richness of coconut milk with lean chicken and fresh herbs, offering a satisfying and nourishing dinner option.

Ingredients

- 1 lb chicken breast, thinly sliced
- 1 can (14 oz) light coconut milk
- 3 cups low-sodium chicken broth
- 1-inch piece of ginger, sliced
- 2 cloves garlic, minced
- 1 tbsp olive oil   ;1/4 cup lime juice
- 1 stalk lemongrass, smashed
- 1 tbsp fish sauce (option

Direction

1. Heat olive oil in a large pot. Add garlic, ginger, and lemongrass, sautéing for 2 minutes until fragrant.
2. Add chicken broth and coconut milk, bringing to a gentle simmer. Add chicken slices and cook for 10-12 minutes until fully cooked.
3. Stir in mushrooms, spinach, lime juice, and fish sauce. Cook for another 2-3 minutes.
4. Remove lemongrass stalk before serving. Garnish with cilantro.

Nutritional Content (per serving)	Storage Tips	Cooking and Ingredients Tips
<ul><li>Calories: 280 kcal</li><li>Total Fat: 15g</li><li>Protein: 25g</li><li>Carbohydrates: 12g</li><li>Sugars: 3g</li><li>Fiber: 3g</li><li>Sodium: 290mg</li></ul>	Store in the refrigerator for up to 4 days. This soup can also be frozen without the spinach for up to 3 months.	<ul><li>For a spicier version, add a few slices of fresh chili.</li><li>To cut down on fat, use half the amount of coconut milk and replace it with extra broth.</li></ul>

Chapter Five

Chicken & Turkey Based Meals

GRILLED CHICKEN WITH QUINOA

A simple yet flavorful grilled chicken dish with a side of quinoa, rich in protein and fiber, perfect for a low-GI, diabetic-friendly meal.

Cooking Details

Prep 10 (Mins)

Time 20 (Mins)

Serves 4

Ingredients

- 4 boneless, skinless chicken breasts
- 2 tbsp olive oil
- 1 tbsp lemon zest
- 2 tbsp fresh lemon juice
- 2 cloves garlic, minced
- 1 tsp dried oregano
- 1 cup quinoa
- 2 cups low-sodium chicken brot

Direction

1. In a small bowl, mix olive oil, lemon zest, lemon juice, garlic, and oregano. Marinate chicken in this mixture for 15-20 minutes.
2. While marinating, cook quinoa in chicken broth by bringing it to a boil and then simmering for 15 minutes until tender.
3. Grill the marinated chicken on medium heat for 6-7 minutes per side, until fully cooked.
4. Serve chicken over quinoa and garnish with fresh parsley.

Nutritional Content (per serving)	Storage Tips	Cooking and Ingredients Tips
- Calories: 320 kcal - Total Fat: 10g - Protein: 38g - Carbohydrates: 25g - Sugars: 1g - Fiber: 3g - Sodium: 150mg	Store grilled chicken and cooked quinoa in separate airtight containers in the fridge for up to 3 days.	- For extra flavor, marinate the chicken for up to 2 hours. - Quinoa can be swapped for another whole grain like brown rice or farro if preferred.

TURKEY AND SPINACH STUFFED BELL PEPPERS

These colorful bell peppers are filled with a savory turkey and spinach mixture, offering a hearty and nutritious low-carb meal that's rich in fiber and protein.

Cooking Details

Prep 15 (Mins)

Time 25 (Mins)

Serves 4

Ingredients

- 4 large bell peppers (any color), tops cut off and seeds removed
- 1 lb lean ground turkey
- 1 small onion, diced ; 2 cloves garlic, minced
- 1 cup fresh spinach, chopped
- 1/2 cup cooked brown rice
- 1/2 cup low-sodium tomato sauce
- 1 tbsp olive oil ; Salt and pepper to taste

Direction

1. Preheat the oven to 375°F (190°C).
2. Heat olive oil in a skillet. Add onions and garlic, and sauté for 3-4 minutes. Add ground turkey and cook until browned.
3. Stir in spinach, cooked brown rice, and tomato sauce. Season with salt and pepper.
4. Stuff each bell pepper with the turkey mixture. Place in a baking dish and bake for 25 minutes.

Nutritional Content (per serving)	Storage Tips	Cooking and Ingredients Tips
- Calories: 280 kcal - Total Fat: 9g - Protein: 24g - Carbohydrates: 22g - Sugars: 7g - Fiber: 5g - Sodium: 220mg	Store stuffed peppers in an airtight container in the fridge for up to 3 days. To reheat, bake at 350°F (175°C) for 15-20 minutes or microwave until hot.	- For a spicier version, add a few slices of fresh chili. - To cut down on fat, use half the amount of coconut milk and replace it with extra broth.

TURKEY ZUCCHINI MEATBALLS WITH TOMATO BASIL SAUCE

These light and healthy turkey meatballs, mixed with zucchini for extra moisture and fiber, are served in a simple tomato basil sauce for a delicious, diabetic-friendly meal.

Cooking Details
- Prep 15 (Mins)
- Time 25 (Mins)
- Serves 4

Ingredients

- 1 lb ground turkey
- 1 small zucchini, grated
- 1 egg ; 1/4 cup almond flour
- 2 tbsp fresh parsley, chopped
- 1/2 tsp garlic powder
- Salt and pepper to taste
- 2 cups low-sodium tomato sauce
- 1 tbsp olive oil ; Fresh basil for garnish

Direction

1. Preheat oven to 400°F (200°C).
2. In a large bowl, combine ground turkey, grated zucchini, egg, almond flour, parsley, garlic powder, salt, and pepper. Form into meatballs.
3. Place the meatballs on a baking sheet lined with parchment paper and bake for 20 minutes or until cooked through.
4. Heat the tomato sauce with olive oil in a skillet over medium heat for 5 minutes. Serve the meatballs with the tomato basil sauce, garnished with fresh basil.

Nutritional Content (per serving)	Storage Tips	Cooking and Ingredients Tips
• Calories: 280 kcal • Total Fat: 12g • Protein: 30g • Carbohydrates: 14g • Sugars: 6g • Fiber: 4g • Sodium: 300mg	• Store cooked meatballs in an airtight container in the fridge for up to 3 days, or freeze for up to 3 months. Reheat in the microwave or oven until fully warmed.	• Grating zucchini or carrots into the meatballs adds moisture and fiber without affecting the flavor. Almond flour keeps them gluten-free, but regular breadcrumbs can be used if gluten isn't a concern.

CHICKEN STIR-FRY WITH BROCCOLI AND CASHEWS

A quick and healthy stir-fry that brings together lean chicken, fiber-rich broccoli, and heart-healthy cashews in a flavorful low-sodium soy sauce glaze.

Cooking Details
- Prep 10 (Mins)
- Time 115 (Mins)
- Serves 4

Ingredients

- 1 lb boneless, skinless chicken breast, sliced
- 2 cups broccoli florets
- 1/2 cup carrots, julienned
- 1/4 cup unsalted cashews
- 2 tbsp low-sodium soy sauce
- 1 tbsp sesame oil ; 1 tbsp olive oil
- 1 clove garlic, minced
- 1 tsp fresh ginger, minced

1. Heat olive oil in a skillet or wok over medium-high heat. Add the chicken slices and cook for 5-6 minutes until browned.
2. Add garlic, ginger, broccoli, and carrots. Stir-fry for 4-5 minutes until the vegetables are tender.
3. Stir in the soy sauce, sesame oil, and cashews. Cook for an additional 2 minutes and serve hot.

Nutritional Content (per serving)	Storage Tips	Cooking and Ingredients Tips
• Calories: 240 kcal • Total Fat: 14g • Protein: 32g • Carbohydrates: 12g • Sugars: 4g • Fiber: 4g • Sodium: 200mg	Store the stir-fry in an airtight container in the fridge for up to 3 days. Reheat on the stovetop or in the microwave until heated through.	For a lower-sodium alternative, use coconut aminos instead of soy sauce. You can add other vegetables like snap peas, bell peppers, or mushrooms for more variety and color.

BAKED TURKEY CUTLETS WITH SWEET POTATO MASH

Tender baked turkey cutlets paired with creamy sweet potato mash, offering a balanced mix of protein, healthy carbs, and fiber.

Cooking Details

- Prep 15 (Mins)
- Time 35 (Mins)
- Serves 4

Ingredients

For the Turkey Cutlets:
- 4 turkey cutlets (about 4 oz each, trimmed of fat)
- 1 tbsp olive oil
- 1 tsp garlic powder
- 1 tsp dried thyme
- 1/2 tsp smoked paprika
- salt (To taste)
- 1/4 tsp black pepper

For the Sweet Potato Mash:
- 2 large sweet potatoes, peeled and cubed
- 2 tbsp unsweetened almond milk
- 1 tbsp olive oil
- 1/2 tsp cinnamon
- 1/4 tsp nutmeg (optional)
- 1/8 tsp salt

Direction

1. Preheat the oven to 375°F (190°C) &line baking sheet with parchment paper.
2. Rub turkey cutlets with olive oil, then season with garlic powder, thyme, smoked paprika, salt, and pepper. Place the cutlets on the baking sheet.
3. Bake for 20-25 minutes, flipping halfway through, until the internal temperature reaches 165°F (74°C).
4. While the turkey bakes, place cubed sweet potatoes in a medium pot. Cover with water, bring to a boil, and cook for 12-15 minutes until tender.
5. Mash Sweet Potatoes: Drain the cooked sweet potatoes and mash with almond milk, olive oil, cinnamon, nutmeg, and a pinch of salt until smooth. Adjust seasoning to taste.

Nutritional Content (per serving)	Storage Tips	Cooking and Ingredients Tips
- Calories: 280 kcal - Total Fat: 8 g - Protein: 28 g - Carbohydrates: 25 g - Sugars: 6 g - Fiber: 4 g - Sodium: 260 mg	Store leftovers in an airtight container in the fridge for up to 3 days. Sweet potato mash can be frozen in freezer-safe containers for up to 2 months. Turkey cutlets can be frozen for 3 months.	- Ensure even thickness for uniform cooking. If cutlets are uneven, pound them gently to flatten. - Choose sweet potatoes with smooth skin and deep orange flesh for the best flavor and nutritional value. - Cinnamon may help regulate blood sugar levels due to its potential insulin-sensitizing properties

---

HERB-ROASTED CHICKEN WITH ROOT VEGETABLES

This oven-roasted chicken is seasoned with fragrant herbs and paired with nutrient-dense root vegetables like carrots and parsnips for a balanced, diabetic-friendly dinner.

Cooking Details

- Prep 15 (Mins)
- Time   (Mins)
- Serves 4

Ingredients

- 4 bone-in, skinless chicken thighs
- 2 tbsp olive oil ; 2 tsp dried rosemary
- 1 tsp dried thyme
- 3 carrots, peeled and cut into chunks
- 2 parsnips, peeled and cut into chunks
- 1 red onion, cut into wedges
- Salt and pepper to taste

Direction

1. Preheat oven to 400°F (200°C).
2. Toss the vegetables with 1 tbsp of olive oil, rosemary, thyme, salt, and pepper. Arrange in a baking dish.
3. Rub the chicken thighs with the remaining olive oil and season with salt and pepper. Place on top of the vegetables.
4. Roast for 40-45 minutes, or until the chicken reaches an internal temperature of 165°F (75°C) and the vegetables are tender.

Nutritional Content (per serving)	Storage Tips	Cooking and Ingredients Tips
- Calories: 380 kcal - Total Fat: 18g - Protein: 28g - Carbohydrates: 25g - Sugars: 8g - Fiber: 6g - Sodium: 200mg	Store roasted chicken and vegetables in an airtight container in the fridge for up to 3 days.	For extra crispiness, roast the chicken thighs without the skin. You can also use chicken breasts if preferred. Other root vegetables like sweet potatoes or turnips can be added for variety.

GROUND TURKEY LETTUCE WRAPS

These light and flavorful lettuce wraps feature ground turkey cooked with ginger and soy sauce, offering a low-carb, diabetic-friendly alternative to traditional wraps.

Cooking Details

📖 Prep 10 (Mins)

🕐 Time 15 (Mins)

🍴 Serves 4

Ingredients

- 1 lb ground turkey
- 1 small zucchini, grated
- 1 egg ; 1/4 cup almond flour
- 2 tbsp fresh parsley, chopped
- 1/2 tsp garlic powder
- Salt and pepper to taste
- 2 cups low-sodium tomato sauce
- 1 tbsp olive oil
- Fresh basil for garnish

Direction

1. Sauté minced garlic, ginger, and diced onions in a skillet with olive oil until fragrant.
2. Add ground turkey and cook until browned, breaking it into small pieces as it cooks.
3. Stir in soy sauce, hoisin sauce, and a splash of rice vinegar. Cook until the turkey absorbs the flavors.
4. Add diced water chestnuts and chopped green onions, cooking briefly for added crunch.
5. Wash and separate large lettuce leaves for wraps.
6. Spoon the turkey mixture into the lettuce leaves and serve immediately, garnished with sesame seeds or chili flakes if desired.

Nutritional Content (per serving)	Storage Tips	Cooking and Ingredients Tips
- Calories: 220 kcal - Total Fat: 12g - Protein: 26g - Carbohydrates: 6g - Sugars: 2g - Fiber: 2g - Sodium: 250mg	Store the turkey filling in an airtight container in the fridge for up to 3 days. Lettuce should be stored separately to maintain crispness.	You can add water chestnuts or mushrooms for added texture in the filling. Butter lettuce or iceberg lettuce can also be used for the wraps.

TURKEY CHILI WITH BLACK BEANS

This hearty turkey chili is packed with lean protein, black beans, and spices, making it a perfect warm, diabetic-friendly meal on cold days.

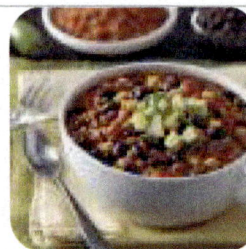

Cooking Details

📖 Prep 10 (Mins)

🕐 Time 30 (Mins)

🍴 Serves 4

Ingredients

- 1 lb lean ground turkey
- 1 can (15 oz) black beans, rinsed and drained
- 1 can (15 oz) diced tomatoes, no salt added
- 1 small onion, diced; 2 cloves garlic, minced
- 1 tbsp chili powder
- 1 tsp cumin ;1 tsp paprika
- 1 tbsp olive oil

Direction

1. Sauté onions, garlic, and bell peppers in olive oil until softened.
2. Cook ground turkey until browned and fully cooked.
3. Add chili powder, cumin, smoked paprika, oregano, salt, and pepper, and cook briefly to release flavors.
4. Stir in diced tomatoes, tomato paste, black beans, and chicken broth or water.
5. Simmer the chili on low heat for 20-25 minutes, stirring occasionally, until thickened.
6. Adjust seasoning to taste and serve with your choice of toppings like cilantro, avocado, cheese, or Greek yogurt.

Nutritional Content (per serving)	Storage Tips	Cooking and Ingredients Tips
- Calories: 290 kcal - Total Fat: 10g - Protein: 30g - Carbohydrates: 24g - Sugars: 4g - Fiber: 8g - Sodium: 300mg	- Store the stir-fry in an airtight container in the fridge for up to 3 days. Reheat on the stovetop or in the microwave until heated through.	- If you want a spicier chili, add a pinch of cayenne pepper or chopped jalapeños. - You can substitute kidney beans or pinto beans if you prefer.

GRILLED TURKEY BURGERS WITH AVOCADO

These lean turkey burgers are topped with creamy avocado for a satisfying, heart-healthy, and diabetic-friendly meal.

Ingredients

- 1 lb ground turkey
- 1/4 cup almond flour
- 1 egg
- 1/2 tsp garlic powder
- 1/2 tsp onion powder
- Salt and pepper to taste
- 1 avocado, sliced
- 4 whole grain burger buns (or lettuce wraps)

Direction

1. Heat the grill to medium-high (375°F to 400°F).
2. In a bowl, combine ground turkey, breadcrumbs, grated onion, minced garlic, salt, pepper, and smoked paprika. Mix gently.
3. Shape the mixture into four patties, making an indentation in the center.
4. Cook the patties on the grill for 5-6 minutes per side, until the internal temperature reaches 165°F.
5. Optionally, toast whole grain buns on the grill for the last minute.
6. Place each patty on a bun or lettuce wrap and top with avocado
7. Serve

Nutritional Content (per serving)	Storage Tips	Cooking and Ingredients Tips
- Calories: 340 kcal - Total Fat: 16g - Protein: 28g - Carbohydrates: 24g - Sugars: 2g - Fiber: 5g - Sodium: 280mg	- Store cooked turkey patties in the fridge for up to 3 days. Reheat in the microwave or stovetop. - Avocado should be added fresh to prevent browning.	For added flavor, mix in fresh herbs like parsley or cilantro into the burger mixture. For a lighter option, serve the burgers in lettuce wraps instead of buns.

CHICKEN AND VEGETABLE SKEWERS

Colorful skewers loaded with chicken and vegetables, grilled to perfection, make for a delicious, balanced, and diabetic-friendly dinner.

Ingredients

- 1 lb boneless, skinless chicken breast, cubed
- 1 zucchini, sliced
- 1 red bell pepper, chopped
- 1 red onion, chopped
- 1 tbsp olive oil ; 1 tsp dried oregano
- 1 tsp paprika
- Salt and pepper to taste

Direction

1. Preheat the grill to medium heat.
2. Toss chicken cubes and vegetables with olive oil, oregano, paprika, salt, and pepper.
3. Thread chicken and vegetables onto skewers, alternating between each ingredient.
4. Grill skewers for 12-15 minutes, turning occasionally, until chicken is fully cooked.

Nutritional Content (per serving)	Storage Tips	Cooking and Ingredients Tips
- Calories: 270 kcal - Total Fat: 10g - Protein: 30g - Carbohydrates: 12g - Sugars: 5g - Fiber: 3g - Sodium: 240mg	- Store the cooked chicken and vegetable skewers in the fridge for up to 3 days.	Wooden skewers should be soaked in water for 30 minutes before grilling to prevent burning. You can add mushrooms, cherry tomatoes, or pineapple chunks to the skewers for more variety.

Chapter Six

Meatless Main Dishes

LENTIL & SPINACH STEW

This hearty lentil and spinach stew is a comforting, protein-packed, meatless meal with fiber and essential vitamins, perfect for managing blood sugar and supporting digestive health.

Cooking Details

Prep   10 (Mins)
Time   40 (Mins)
Serves   4

Ingredients

- 1 cup dried lentils, rinsed
- 4 cups vegetable broth (low-sodium)
- 1 small onion, diced
- 2 cloves garlic, minced
- 1 can (15 oz) diced tomatoes, no salt added
- 2 cups fresh spinach
- 1 tsp cumin;   1 tsp paprika
- 1 tbsp olive oil;Salt and pepper to taste

Direction

1. Heat olive oil in a large pot over medium heat. Sauté onions and garlic for 3-4 minutes until softened.
2. Add lentils, vegetable broth, diced tomatoes, cumin, and paprika. Bring to a boil, then reduce heat and simmer for 30 minutes.
3. Stir in fresh spinach during the last 5 minutes of cooking. Season with salt and pepper.
4. Serve warm with a slice of whole-grain bread, if desired.

Nutritional Content (per serving)	Storage Tips	Cooking and Ingredients Tips
• Calories: 280 kcal • Total Fat: 5g • Protein: 15g • Carbohydrates: 43g • Sugars: 8g • Fiber: 14g • Sodium: 380mg	Store in an airtight container in the fridge for up to 4 days, or freeze for up to 3 months. Reheat on the stovetop or in the microwave.	For extra protein, you can add cubed tofu or chickpeas. Use baby spinach for convenience; it wilts quickly into the stew.

QUINOA-STUFFED BELL PEPPERS

These colorful bell peppers are stuffed with a flavorful quinoa and vegetable mixture, offering a nutrient-rich, low-GI, meatless option to support balanced blood sugar levels.

Cooking Details

Prep   15 (Mins)
Time   30 (Mins)
Serves   4

Ingredients

- 4 large bell peppers, tops cut off
- 1 cup quinoa, rinsed
- 1 1/2 cups vegetable broth (low-sodium)
- 1 small zucchini, diced
- 1/2 cup corn kernels (fresh or frozen)
- 1/2 cup diced tomatoes, no salt added
- 1 tsp dried oregano ; 1 tbsp olive oil
- Salt and pepper to taste

Direction

1. Heat oven to 375°F (190°C).
2. Prepare quinoa in vegetable broth as per package instructions (about 15 minutes). Set aside.
3. In a skillet, heat olive oil and sauté zucchini for 3-4 minutes. Add corn, diced tomatoes, oregano, salt, and pepper.
4. Combine the cooked quinoa with the vegetable mixture.
5. Fill each bell pepper with the quinoa mixture and place in a baking dish. Bake for 25-30 minutes until peppers are tender.

Nutritional Content (per serving)	Storage Tips	Cooking and Ingredients Tips
• Calories: 290 kcal • Total Fat: 8g • Protein: 9g • Carbohydrates: 45g • Sugars: 10g • Fiber: 8g • Sodium: 230mg	Store stuffed peppers in the fridge for up to 3 days. Reheat in the oven at 350°F for 10-15 minutes or in the microwave.	For added flavor, sprinkle some grated Parmesan or nutritional yeast on top before baking.

TOFU AND VEGETABLE STIR-FRY

This diabetes-friendly meal packed with plant-based protein from tofu and fiber-rich, low-glycemic vegetables like broccoli, bell peppers, and zucchini.

Cooking Details
- Prep 15 (Mins)
- Time 10 (Mins)
- Serves 4

Ingredients

- 1 block firm tofu, pressed and cubed ; 2 cups broccoli florets
- 1 red bell pepper, sliced
- 1 carrot, thinly sliced
- 2 tbsp low-sodium soy sauce
- 1 tbsp sesame oil; 2 cloves garlic
- 1 tbsp grated ginger
- 1 tbsp sesame seeds (optional)
- 1 tbsp olive oil
- Brown rice, cooked, for serving

Direction

1. Heat olive oil in a skillet over medium heat. Add tofu cubes and cook for 4-5 minutes, until lightly browned. Remove from skillet and set aside.
2. In the same skillet, add sesame oil, garlic, and ginger. Sauté for 1 minute.
3. Add broccoli, bell pepper, and carrot. Stir-fry for 5-7 minutes until vegetables are tender-crisp.
4. Stir in the tofu and soy sauce. Cook for 2 more minutes. Sprinkle sesame seeds on top before serving.
5. Serve over cooked brown rice.

Nutritional Content (per serving)	Storage Tips	Cooking and Ingredients Tips
• Calories: 320 kcal • Total Fat: 12g • Protein: 15g • Carbohydrates: 40g • Sugars: 5g • Fiber: 6g • Sodium: 340mg	• Store in the fridge for up to 3 days. Reheat in a skillet or microwave. • Store tofu and vegetables separately from the rice for best texture.	• Pressing tofu before cooking helps remove excess moisture, allowing it to crisp up better. • Add mushrooms or snow peas for extra texture and flavor.

CHICKPEA AND CAULIFLOWER CURRY

This aromatic chickpea and cauliflower curry is full of spices and plant-based protein, offering a satisfying meal that keeps blood sugar levels steady.

Cooking Details
- Prep 10 (Mins)
- Time 25 (Mins)
- Serves 4

Ingredients

- 1 can (15 oz) chickpeas, rinsed and drained
- 1 small head of cauliflower, cut into florets
- 1 small onion, diced
- 1 can (15 oz) light coconut milk
- 1 tbsp curry powder ; 1 tsp turmeric
- 1 tbsp olive oil
- 1 cup diced tomatoes, no salt added
- Fresh cilantro for garnish

Direction

1. Heat olive oil in a large pot over medium heat. Add onions and sauté for 3-4 minutes.
2. Stir in curry powder and turmeric, cooking for 1 minute.
3. Add cauliflower, chickpeas, diced tomatoes, and coconut milk. Bring to a simmer and cook for 15-20 minutes, until the cauliflower is tender.
4. Serve over brown rice or quinoa, garnished with fresh cilantro.

Nutritional Content (per serving)	Storage Tips	Cooking and Ingredients Tips
• Calories: 350 kcal • Total Fat: 12g • Protein: 12g • Carbohydrates: 50g • Sugars: 7g • Fiber: 11g • Sodium: 250mg	Store in the fridge for up to 4 days or freeze for up to 3 months. Reheat in a pot over low heat or in the microwave.	You can swap out cauliflower for broccoli or sweet potatoes for variety. If you prefer a spicier curry, add a pinch of cayenne pepper or red pepper flakes.

BLACK BEAN AND SWEET POTATO TACOS

These vegetarian tacos combine black beans and sweet potatoes for a fiber-rich, flavorful meal that's perfect for seniors looking to maintain stable blood sugar levels.

Ingredients

- 1 medium sweet potato, diced
- 1 can (15 oz) black beans, rinsed and drained
- 1/2 tsp cumin
- 1/2 tsp smoked paprika
- 1 tbsp olive oil
- Corn or whole wheat tortillas
- 1/4 cup chopped red onion
- Fresh cilantro and lime wedges

Direction

1. Preheat oven to 400°F (200°C).
2. Toss diced sweet potatoes with olive oil, cumin, and smoked paprika. Spread on a baking sheet and roast for 20 minutes, until tender.
3. Warm black beans in a small pot over low heat.
4. Assemble tacos by layering black beans and roasted sweet potatoes on tortillas. Top with chopped red onion, cilantro, and a squeeze of lime.

Nutritional Content (per serving)	Storage Tips	Cooking and Ingredients Tips
- Calories: 280 kcal - Total Fat: 6g - Protein: 9g - Carbohydrates: 50g - Sugars: 7g - Fiber: 10g - Sodium: 180mg	Store roasted sweet potatoes and beans separately in airtight containers for up to 3 days. Reheat and assemble when ready to eat.	You can add a dollop of Greek yogurt or guacamole for extra creaminess. Use corn tortillas for a gluten-free option.

SPINACH AND MUSHROOM FRITTATA

This protein-packed frittata combines spinach and mushrooms, making it a light, diabetic-friendly meal that's perfect for breakfast or lunch.

Ingredients

- 6 large eggs
- 2 cups fresh spinach
- 1 cup mushrooms, sliced
- 1/4 cup low-fat feta cheese
- 1/4 cup milk (or plant-based milk)
- 1 tbsp olive oil
- Salt and pepper to taste

Direction

1. Preheat oven to 350°F (175°C).
2. In a skillet, heat olive oil and sauté mushrooms for 3-4 minutes. Add spinach and cook until wilted.
3. In a bowl, whisk eggs, milk, salt, and pepper. Stir in sautéed vegetables.
4. Pour the mixture into an oven-safe skillet or baking dish. Top with feta cheese.
5. Bake for 15-20 minutes.

Nutritional Content (per serving)	Storage Tips	Cooking and Ingredients Tips
- Calories: 230 kcal - Total Fat: 14g - Protein: 16g - Carbohydrates: 6g - Sugars: 3g - Fiber: 2g - Sodium: 300mg	Store leftovers in the fridge for up to 3 days. Reheat in the oven or microwave.	- You can add other vegetables like bell peppers or tomatoes for extra flavor. - Substitute dairy-free cheese if preferred.

MEDITERRANEAN CHICKPEA SALAD

A refreshing and colorful chickpea salad filled with Mediterranean flavors, rich in fiber, healthy fats, and plant-based protein. This dish helps balance blood sugar while promoting heart health.

Cooking Details

📋 Prep 15 (Mins)
🕐 Time n/d (Mins)
🍴 Serves 4

Ingredients

- 1 can (15 oz) chickpeas, rinsed and drained
- 1 cup cucumber, diced
- 1 cup cherry tomatoes, halved
- 1/4 cup red onion, finely chopped
- 1/4 cup Kalamata olives, chopped
- 1/4 cup crumbled feta cheese
- 2 tbsp olive oil ; 1 tbsp lemon juice
- 1 tsp dried oregano
- Salt and pepper to taste

Direction

1. In a large bowl, combine chickpeas, cucumber, tomatoes, red onion, and olives.
2. In a small bowl, whisk together olive oil, lemon juice, oregano, salt, and pepper.
3. Pour the dressing over the chickpea mixture and toss gently.
4. Top with crumbled feta cheese and fresh parsley. Serve immediately or chilled.

Nutritional Content (per serving)	Storage Tips	Cooking and Ingredients Tips
<ul><li>Calories: 290 kcal</li><li>Total Fat: 14g</li><li>Protein: 10g</li><li>Carbohydrates: 28g</li><li>Sugars: 6g</li><li>Fiber: 8g</li><li>Sodium: 380mg</li></ul>	Store in an airtight container in the fridge for up to 3 days. Toss before serving to redistribute the dressing	<ul><li>Use fresh herbs like parsley or basil for extra flavor.</li><li>Substitute feta cheese with a dairy-free alternative for a vegan version.</li></ul>

CREAMY COCONUT CAULIFLOWER RICE BOWL

This low-carb, diabetic-friendly coconut cauliflower rice bowl is creamy, filling, and packed with anti-inflammatory spices. It's an excellent alternative to traditional rice dishes.

Cooking Details

📋 Prep 10 (Mins)
🕐 Time 15 (Mins)
🍴 Serves 4

Ingredients

- 1 medium head of cauliflower, grated
- 1/2 cup light coconut milk
- 1 tsp turmeric ; 1 tsp cumin
- 1 tbsp olive oil ; Salt and pepper to taste
- 1 cup green peas (fresh or frozen)
- 1/2 cup shredded carrots

Direction

1. Heat olive oil in a large skillet over medium heat. Add cauliflower rice and sauté for 3-4 minutes.
2. Stir in coconut milk, turmeric, cumin, salt, and pepper. Cook for another 5 minutes until cauliflower rice is tender.
3. Add green peas and shredded carrots, cooking for an additional 2-3 minutes until vegetables are warmed through.
4. Garnish with fresh cilantro before serving.

Nutritional Content (per serving)	Storage Tips	Cooking and Ingredients Tips
<ul><li>Calories: 190 kcal</li><li>Total Fat: 9g</li><li>Protein: 5g</li><li>Carbohydrates: 20g</li><li>Sugars: 6g</li><li>Fiber: 6g</li><li>Sodium: 220mg</li></ul>	<ul><li>Store in an airtight container in the fridge for up to 3 days. Reheat gently in a skillet to maintain texture.</li></ul>	<ul><li>You can substitute frozen cauliflower rice for convenience.</li><li>Add diced tofu or chickpeas for extra protein.</li></ul>

ZUCCHINI NOODLES WITH PESTO

A light and flavorful dish of zucchini noodles tossed in a creamy, nutrient-dense pesto sauce made from spinach and nuts. This low-carb meal is great for seniors managing diabetes.

Cooking Details
Prep 15 (Mins)
Time 5 (Mins)
Serves 4

Ingredients

- 4 medium zucchini, spiralized into noodles
- 2 cups fresh spinach
- 1/4 cup walnuts or almonds
- 1/4 cup Parmesan cheese (optional)
- 1/4 cup olive oil
- 2 cloves garlic
- 1 tbsp lemon juice
- Salt and pepper to taste

Direction

1. Spiralize Zucchini: Use a spiralizer to create zucchini noodles.
2. Cook Noodles: Sauté the zucchini noodles in a skillet with olive oil for 2-3 minutes until slightly tender.
3. Add Pesto: Toss the noodles with your favorite pesto sauce until evenly coated.
4. Serve: Plate and garnish with grated Parmesan cheese or toasted pine nuts, if desired.

Nutritional Content (per serving)	Storage Tips	Cooking and Ingredients Tips
• Calories: 230 kcal • Total Fat: 19g • Protein: 6g • Carbohydrates: 11g • Sugars: 4g • Fiber: 4g • Sodium: 180mg	Store zucchini noodles and pesto separately in the fridge for up to 3 days. Reheat zucchini noodles gently and toss with pesto just before serving.	Swap spinach for basil if you prefer a more traditional pesto. Use pre-spiralized zucchini for a quicker prep time.

MUSHROOM AND BARLEY RISOTTO

A creamy and satisfying barley risotto loaded with mushrooms. Barley is a low-GI grain that provides steady energy, making this dish ideal for blood sugar management.

Cooking Details
Prep 15 (Mins)
Time 45 (Mins)
Serves 4

Ingredients

- 1 cup pearl barley
- 4 cups low-sodium vegetable broth
- 1 cup mushrooms, sliced
- 1 small onion, diced
- 2 cloves garlic, minced
- 1 tbsp olive oil
- 1/4 cup grated Parmesan (optional)
- Fresh parsley for garnish
- Salt and pepper to taste

Direction

1. In a large pot, heat olive oil over medium heat. Add onions and garlic, sautéing for 3-4 minutes until softened.
2. Add sliced mushrooms and cook for another 5 minutes.
3. Stir in the barley and 1 cup of vegetable broth. Cook, stirring frequently, until the broth is absorbed. Continue adding broth, 1 cup at a time, until barley is tender (about 40 minutes).
4. Stir in Parmesan if using, and season with salt and pepper. Serve.

Nutritional Content (per serving)	Storage Tips	Cooking and Ingredients Tips
• Calories: 320 kcal • Total Fat: 9g • Protein: 9g • Carbohydrates: 54g • Sugars: 4g • Fiber: 9g • Sodium: 250mg	• Store in an airtight container in the fridge for up to 3 days. Reheat with a splash of broth or water to bring back the creamy texture.	• You can substitute barley with farro or brown rice if preferred. • For added protein, stir in cooked lentils or chickpeas at the end.

Chapter Seven

Glucose Goddess Desserts

CHIA SEED PUDDING WITH ALMOND MILK

A creamy, fiber-rich dessert packed with omega-3s and protein. Chia seeds absorb liquid to form a pudding-like consistency, making this a perfect low-carb, diabetic-friendly treat

Ingredients

- 1/4 cup chia seeds
- 1 1/2 cups unsweetened almond milk
- 1 tbsp pure maple syrup or sugar-free sweetener
- 1/2 tsp vanilla extract
- Fresh berries for topping (optional)

Direction

1. In a bowl, whisk together almond milk, chia seeds, maple syrup, and vanilla extract.
2. Cover and refrigerate for at least 4 hours or overnight until thickened.
3. Stir well before serving and top with fresh berries.

Nutritional Content (per serving)	Storage Tips	Cooking and Ingredients Tips
• Calories: 110 kcal • Total Fat: 7g • Protein: 4g • Carbohydrates: 10g • Sugars: 2g • Fiber: 8g • Sodium: 60mg	• Store in an airtight container in the fridge for up to 4 days. Stir before serving each time.	• For a creamier texture, use coconut milk instead of almond milk. • Add cinnamon or nutmeg for extra flavor without added sugars.

BAKED APPLE WITH CINNAMON AND WALNUTS

A warm, comforting dessert with natural sweetness from baked apples, complemented by crunchy walnuts and cinnamon.

Ingredients

- 2 medium apples, cored
- 2 tbsp chopped walnuts
- 1/2 tsp cinnamon
- 1 tsp melted butter
- 1 tsp pure maple syrup (optional)

Direction

1. Preheat oven to 350°F (175°C).
2. Place apples in a small baking dish. In a bowl, combine chopped walnuts, cinnamon, melted butter, and maple syrup (if using).
3. Fill the apples with the walnut mixture.
4. Bake for 25 minutes until the apples are tender.

Nutritional Content (per serving)	Storage Tips	Cooking and Ingredients Tips
• Calories: 160 kcal • Total Fat: 7g • Protein: 2g • Carbohydrates: 24g • Sugars: 16g • Fiber: 5g • Sodium: 10mg	• Store baked apples in an airtight container in the fridge for up to 2 days. Reheat in the microwave for 20 seconds before serving.	• Use a variety of apple like Granny Smith or Gala for different flavors and textures. • You can replace walnuts with pecans for a different nutty twist.

GREEK YOGURT AND BERRY PARFAIT

A light and refreshing dessert made with creamy Greek yogurt and antioxidant-rich berries. This parfait is an excellent source of protein and is naturally low in sugar.

Cooking Details

Prep 10 (Mins)
Time n/d(Mins)
Serves 4

Ingredients

- 2 cups plain, unsweetened Greek yogurt
- 1 cup mixed berries (blueberries, strawberries, raspberries)
- 1 tbsp slivered almonds
- 1 tsp honey (optional)

Direction

1. Layer Yogurt: Add a layer of plain Greek yogurt to a glass or bowl.
2. Add Berries: Top with a layer of fresh mixed berries (like blueberries, strawberries, or raspberries).
3. Repeat Layers: Repeat the layers of yogurt and berries until the glass is filled.
4. Top and Serve: Finish with a sprinkle of chopped nuts, seeds, or unsweetened granola for added crunch. Serve immediately.

Nutritional Content (per serving)	Storage Tips	Cooking and Ingredients Tips
• Calories: 150 kcal • Total Fat: 5g • Protein: 10g • Carbohydrates: 12g • Sugars: 6g • Fiber: 4g • Sodium: 55mg	• Store parfaits in the fridge for up to 2 days. Keep toppings (like almonds) separate until ready to serve to maintain crunchiness.	• Use unsweetened coconut yogurt for a dairy-free option. • Substitute chia seeds with ground flaxseeds for similar nutritional benefits.

AVOCADO CHOCOLATE MOUSSE

A creamy, rich chocolate mousse made with avocado, offering a healthy dose of monounsaturated fats and antioxidants. It's an indulgent dessert that's still diabetic-friendly.

Cooking Details

Prep 10 (Mins)
Time n/d(Mins)
Serves 2

Ingredients

- 2 ripe avocados
- 1/4 cup unsweetened cocoa powder
- 1/4 cup unsweetened almond milk
- 2 tbsp maple syrup or sugar-free sweetener
- 1 tsp vanilla extract
- Dark chocolate shavings for garnish (optional)

Direction

1. In a food processor, blend avocados, cocoa powder, almond milk, maple syrup, and vanilla extract until smooth.
2. Transfer the mousse to individual bowls and chill in the fridge for at least 30 minutes.
3. Garnish with dark chocolate shavings if desired before serving.

Nutritional Content (per serving)	Storage Tips	Cooking and Ingredients Tips
• Calories: 170 kcal • Total Fat: 12g • Protein: 3g • Carbohydrates: 16g • Sugars: 6g • Fiber: 8g • Sodium: 15mg	• Store the mousse in the fridge for up to 2 days. Cover tightly to prevent browning of the avocado.	• For a more intense chocolate flavor, add a pinch of espresso powder. • Use cacao powder for an even richer taste and more antioxidants.

COCONUT MACAROONS

Chewy and naturally sweetened coconut macaroons made with unsweetened shredded coconut and egg whites. These treats are low in sugar and perfect for a quick dessert.

Cooking Details

- Prep 12 (Mins)
- Time 10 (Mins)
- Serves 20

Ingredients

- 2 cups unsweetened shredded coconut
- 3 egg whites
- 1/4 cup sugar-free sweetener or coconut sugar
- 1 tsp vanilla extract
- A pinch of salt

Direction

1. Preheat oven to 325°F (165°C) and line a baking sheet with parchment paper.
2. In a bowl, beat egg whites until frothy. Add sweetener, vanilla, and salt, then fold in shredded coconut.
3. Scoop tablespoons of the mixture onto the baking sheet and bake for 20 minutes or until golden brown.
4. Cool before serving.

Nutritional Content (per serving)	Storage Tips	Cooking and Ingredients Tips
- Calories: 70 kcal - Total Fat: 6g - Protein: 2g - Carbohydrates: 3g - Sugars: 1g - Fiber: 2g - Sodium: 20mg	- Store in an airtight container at room temperature for up to 3 days or refrigerate for up to 5 days	- For a chocolate twist, dip the bottom of each macaroon in melted dark chocolate and let it set. - Make sure to use unsweetened coconut to keep the recipe diabetic-friendly.

ALMOND FLOUR BANANA BREAD

A moist, low-carb banana bread made with almond flour and naturally sweetened with ripe bananas. Perfect for seniors who want a guilt-free, diabetes-friendly dessert.

Cooking Details

- Prep 10 (Mins)
- Time 40 (Mins)
- Serves 10

Ingredients

- 2 ripe bananas, mashed
- 1 1/2 cups almond flour
- 2 large eggs
- 1/4 cup sugar-free sweetener
- 1 tsp vanilla extract
- 1 tsp baking soda
- 1/4 tsp cinnamon
- A pinch of salt

Direction

1. Preheat oven to 350°F (175°C) and line a loaf pan with parchment paper.
2. In a bowl, combine mashed bananas, eggs, sweetener, vanilla, and salt.
3. Add almond flour, baking soda, and cinnamon. Stir until well combined.
4. Pour the batter into the loaf pan and bake for 40 minutes, or until a toothpick comes out clean.
5. Let it cool before slicing.

Nutritional Content (per serving)	Storage Tips	Cooking and Ingredients Tips
- Calories: 140 kcal - Total Fat: 9g - Protein: 5g - Carbohydrates: 12g - Sugars: 4g - Fiber: 3g - Sodium: 120mg	- Store the banana bread in an airtight container at room temperature for up to 3 days or freeze for longer storage.	- For a nut-free option, use oat flour instead of almond flour. - Add walnuts or dark chocolate chips to the batter for extra flavor and texture.

LEMON RICOTTA CHEESECAKE BARS

These light and zesty cheesecake bars are made with ricotta and Greek yogurt, offering a high-protein, low-sugar dessert option for seniors managing diabetes.

Cooking Details

🗒 Prep 12 (Mins)
🕐 Time 15 (Mins)
🍴 Serves 35

Ingredients

- 1 1/2 cups almond flour
- 3 tbsp coconut oil, melted
- 2 tbsp sugar-free sweetener
- 1 cup ricotta cheese
- 1/2 cup plain Greek yogurt
- 2 eggs
- 1/4 cup lemon juice
- Zest of 1 lemon
- 1/2 tsp vanilla extract

Direction

1. Preheat oven to 350°F (175°C) and line an 8x8-inch baking dish with parchment paper.
2. In a bowl, mix almond flour, coconut oil, and sweetener to form a crust. Press the mixture into the baking dish.
3. Bake the crust for 10 minutes and set aside.
4. In another bowl, whisk together ricotta, Greek yogurt, eggs, lemon juice, lemon zest, and vanilla until smooth.
5. Pour the filling over the crust and bake for 25 minutes or until the center is set.
6. Let the bars cool before cutting into squares.

Nutritional Content (per serving)	Storage Tips	Cooking and Ingredients Tips
- Calories: 150 kcal - Total Fat: 10g - Protein: 5g - Carbohydrates: 9g - Sugars: 2g - Fiber: 2g - Sodium: 50mg	- Store in the fridge for up to 4 days in an airtight container or freeze individual bars for up to a month.	- For a dairy-free option, substitute ricotta and Greek yogurt with a plant-based alternative like coconut yogurt. - Add a pinch of turmeric for extra color without altering the flavor.

BERRY OAT CRUMBLE

This warm, fiber-rich dessert combines the natural sweetness of berries with a crunchy oat and almond topping, perfect for satisfying a sweet tooth without spiking blood sugar levels.

Cooking Details

🗒 Prep 10 (Mins)
🕐 Time 25 (Mins)
🍴 Serves 6

Ingredients

- 2 cups mixed berries (blueberries, raspberries, strawberries)
- 1/2 cup rolled oats
- 1/4 cup almond flour
- 2 tbsp chopped almonds
- 1 tbsp coconut oil, melted
- 1 tbsp sugar-free sweetener
- 1/2 tsp cinnamon

Direction

1. Preheat oven to 350°F (175°C).
2. Spread berries evenly in a small baking dish.
3. In a bowl, combine oats, almond flour, chopped almonds, coconut oil, sweetener, and cinnamon.
4. Sprinkle the crumble mixture over the berries.
5. Bake for 25 minutes until the topping is golden and the berries are bubbling.

Nutritional Content (per serving)	Storage Tips	Cooking and Ingredients Tips
- Calories: 140 kcal - Total Fat: 6g - Protein: 3g - Carbohydrates: 19g - Sugars: 7g - Fiber: 5g - Sodium: 10mg	Store leftovers in the fridge for up to 3 days. Reheat in the oven or microwave before serving.	- Use frozen berries if fresh ones aren't in season, just allow extra baking time. - For a nut-free version, omit the almonds and use more oats.

DARK CHOCOLATE AVOCADO BROWNIES

Rich, fudgy brownies made with avocado and dark chocolate for a decadent dessert that's low in carbs and high in healthy fats. These are perfect for anyone craving a chocolate treat without the sugar spike.

Ingredients

- 1 ripe avocado, mashed
- 1/2 cup almond flour
- 1/4 cup unsweetened cocoa powder
- 1/4 cup sugar-free sweetener
- 2 eggs ; 1/4 cup dark chocolate chips (optional)
- 1 tsp vanilla extract
- 1/2 tsp baking powder
- A pinch of salt

Direction

1. Preheat oven to 350°F (175°C) and line an 8x8-inch baking pan with parchment paper.
2. In a bowl, whisk together mashed avocado, eggs, sweetener, and vanilla extract; Add almond flour, cocoa powder, baking powder, and salt. Mix until combined.
3. Fold in dark chocolate chips (if using), Pour the batter into the pan and bake for 20 minutes or until a toothpick inserted comes out clean.
4. Let cool before slicing into squares.

Nutritional Content (per serving)	Storage Tips	Cooking and Ingredients Tips
• Calories: 120 kcal • Total Fat: 8g • Protein: 3g • Carbohydrates: 10g • Sugars: 2g • Fiber: 3g • Sodium: 60mg	• Store brownies in an airtight container at room temperature for up to 3 days or freeze for up to 3 months.	• Replace the dark chocolate chips with chopped nuts for added crunch. • Use extra-dark chocolate (85% or higher) for a lower sugar content.

PUMPKIN SPICE MUFFINS

These moist and flavorful muffins use almond flour and pumpkin puree to create a high-fiber, low-carb treat, ideal for seniors managing their blood sugar levels.

Cooking Details
Prep	10 (Mins)
Time	20 (Mins)
Serves	12

Ingredients

- 1 cup almond flour
- 1/2 cup pumpkin puree (unsweetened)
- 2 eggs
- 1/4 cup sugar-free sweetener
- 1 tsp vanilla extract
- 1 tsp baking powder
- 1/2 tsp cinnamon; 1/4 tsp nutmeg
- A pinch of salt

Direction

1. Preheat oven to 350°F (175°C) and line a muffin tin with paper liners.
2. In a bowl, whisk together pumpkin puree, eggs, sweetener, vanilla extract, and a pinch of salt.
3. Add almond flour, baking powder, cinnamon, and nutmeg, and mix until smooth; Divide the batter evenly among the muffin cups.
4. Bake for 20 minutes or until a toothpick inserted in the center comes out clean; Let the muffins cool before serving.

Nutritional Content (per serving)	Storage Tips	Cooking and Ingredients Tips
• Calories: 90 kcal • Total Fat: 6g • Protein: 3g • Carbohydrates: 8g • Sugars: 2g • Fiber: 2g • Sodium: 70mg	Add chopped walnuts or pecans to the batter for extra texture. Substitute almond flour with coconut flour, adjusting the liquid slightly.	• Add chopped walnuts or pecans to the batter for extra texture. • Substitute almond flour with coconut flour, adjusting the liquid slightly.

Chapter Eight

Fish and Seafood

GRILLED SALMON WITH AVOCADO SALSA

This grilled salmon topped with a creamy avocado salsa is high in omega-3 fatty acids, which are heart-healthy and help regulate blood sugar. It's a light, refreshing meal perfect for seniors.

Ingredients

- 4 salmon fillets (6 oz each)
- 2 tbsp olive oil; 1 tsp garlic powder
- 1 tsp paprika
- Salt and black pepper to taste
- Juice of 1 lemon
- 2 ripe avocados, diced
- 1 cup cherry tomatoes, halved
- 1/4 red onion, finely chopped
- 1/4 cup fresh cilantro, chopped
- Juice of 1 lime

Direction

1. Preheat Grill: Heat grill to medium-high (375°F to 400°F).
2. Prepare Salmon: Mix olive oil, garlic powder, paprika, salt, black pepper, and lemon juice in a bowl. Brush over salmon fillets.
3. Grill Salmon: Place salmon skin-side down on the grill. Cook for 5-6 minutes per side, until it flakes easily and reaches 145°F.
4. Make Salsa: In a bowl, combine diced avocados, cherry tomatoes, red onion, cilantro, lime juice, salt, and black pepper. Mix gently.
5. Serve: Top grilled salmon with avocado salsa and enjoy!

Nutritional Content (per serving)	Storage Tips	Cooking and Ingredients Tips
- Calories: 300 kcal - Total Fat: 20g - Protein: 25g - Carbohydrates: 6g - Sugars: 1g - Fiber: 3g - Sodium: 150mg	Store leftover salmon and salsa separately in airtight containers in the fridge for up to 2 days. Reheat the salmon gently in the oven or eat cold in a salad.	Opt for wild-caught salmon, which has a higher omega-3 content. Use lemon juice if lime is unavailable.

BAKED COD WITH GARLIC AND HERBS

This tender baked cod is infused with garlic and fresh herbs, making it a simple yet flavorful dish. It's low in carbs and sodium, making it ideal for blood pressure and blood sugar management.

Ingredients

- 4 cod fillets (about 4 oz each)
- 2 tbsp olive oil
- 3 cloves garlic, minced
- 1 tsp dried thyme
- 1 tsp dried parsley
- Juice of 1 lemon
- Salt and pepper to taste

Direction

1. Preheat the oven to 400°F (200°C).
2. Place the cod fillets in a baking dish. Drizzle with olive oil and lemon juice, and sprinkle with garlic, thyme, parsley, salt, and pepper.
3. Bake for 12-15 minutes until the fish flakes easily with a fork.
4. Serve with a side of steamed vegetables or a fresh salad

Nutritional Content (per serving)	Storage Tips	Cooking and Ingredients Tips
- Calories: 180 kcal - Total Fat: 10g - Protein: 22g - Carbohydrates: 2g - Sugars: 0g - Fiber: 0g - Sodium: 160mg	Store leftovers in an airtight container in the fridge for up to 3 days. Reheat in the oven for best results.	Choose fresh cod fillets, but frozen cod can be used as well—just thaw before cooking. Add fresh herbs like dill or rosemary for additional flavor.

SHRIMP AND ZUCCHINI NOODLES WITH PESTO

A light and low-carb meal featuring shrimp and zucchini noodles tossed in a delicious pesto sauce. It's packed with protein and healthy fats, making it perfect for seniors with diabetes.

Ingredients

- 1 lb large shrimp, peeled and deveined
- 2 tbsp olive oil
- 4 medium zucchinis, spiralized into noodles
- 1/4 cup prepared pesto (low sodium)
- 1 clove garlic, minced
- Juice of 1 lemon
- Salt and pepper to taste

Direction

1. Heat olive oil in a large pan over medium heat. Add shrimp and garlic, and sauté for 3-4 minutes until shrimp are pink and cooked through.
2. Add zucchini noodles to the pan and cook for 2-3 minutes until slightly tender.
3. Remove from heat and toss with pesto and lemon juice. Season with salt and pepper.
4. Serve immediately.

Nutritional Content (per serving)	Storage Tips	Cooking and Ingredients Tips
• Calories: 220 kcal • Total Fat: 14g • Protein: 20g • Carbohydrates: 6g • Sugars: 2g • Fiber: 2g • Sodium: 250mg	Store leftovers in an airtight container in the fridge for up to 2 days. Reheat gently on the stovetop.	Use homemade pesto to control the sodium content or find a store-bought low-sodium option. Zucchini noodles can be substituted with spaghetti squash for variety.

TUNA AND WHITE BEAN SALAD

This no-cook salad is a refreshing, protein-packed option with fiber-rich white beans and healthy fats from olive oil and tuna, great for balancing blood sugar.

Ingredients

- 2 cans tuna in water, drained (5 oz each)
- 1 can white beans, drained and rinsed (15 oz); 1/4 red onion, finely chopped
- 1/2 cup cherry tomatoes, halved
- 1 tbsp olive oil; 1 tbsp red wine vinegar
- 1 tsp Dijon mustard
- Salt and pepper to taste
- Fresh parsley for garnish

Direction

1. In a large bowl, combine tuna, white beans, onion, and cherry tomatoes.
2. In a small bowl, whisk together olive oil, vinegar, mustard, salt, and pepper.
3. Pour the dressing over the tuna mixture and toss to combine.
4. Garnish with fresh parsley and serve.

Nutritional Content (per serving)	Storage Tips	Cooking and Ingredients Tips
• Calories: 180 kcal • Total Fat: 10g • Protein: 22g • Carbohydrates: 2g • Sugars: 0g • Fiber: 0g • Sodium: 160mg	Store in an airtight container in the fridge for up to 3 days. Serve cold or at room temperature.	Use canned tuna packed in water to reduce fat content. Add a handful of arugula or spinach for extra greens.

BAKED TILAPIA WITH LEMON AND ASPARAGUS

This simple baked tilapia with asparagus is low in calories and carbs, but rich in protein and fiber. A perfect quick meal for seniors looking to balance blood sugar and keep sodium in check.

Cooking Details

Prep   10 (Mins)
Time   15   (Mins)
Serves   4

Ingredients

- 4 tilapia fillets (about 4 oz each)
- 1 bunch asparagus, trimmed
- 1 tbsp olive oil
- Juice of 1 lemon
- 1 tsp garlic powder
- Salt and pepper to taste

Direction

1. Preheat oven to 400°F (200°C).
2. Place tilapia fillets and asparagus on a baking sheet lined with parchment paper.
3. Drizzle with olive oil and lemon juice. Sprinkle with garlic powder, salt, and pepper.
4. Bake for 12-15 minutes until the fish is cooked through and asparagus is tender.
5. Serve immediately.

Nutritional Content (per serving)	Storage Tips	Cooking and Ingredients Tips
- Calories: 200 kcal - Total Fat: 7g - Protein: 28g - Carbohydrates: 5g - Sugars: 2g - Fiber: 3g - Sodium: 100mg	Store leftovers in the fridge for up to 2 days. Reheat in the oven or enjoy cold in a salad.	- Substitute tilapia with another white fish like haddock or sole. - Add a sprinkle of paprika or cayenne pepper for a little heat.

GRILLED LEMON GARLIC SHRIMP SKEWERS

These grilled shrimp skewers are a light and flavorful option, rich in protein and low in carbs.

Cooking Details

Prep   15 (Mins)
Time   10 (Mins)
Serves   4

Ingredients

- 1 lb large shrimp, peeled and deveined
- 2 tbsp olive oil
- Juice of 2 lemons
- 3 garlic cloves, minced
- 1 tsp dried oregano
- 1/2 tsp black pepper
- Fresh parsley, for garnish

Direction

1. In a bowl, combine olive oil, lemon juice, garlic, oregano, and black pepper. Toss shrimp in the marinade and refrigerate for at least 30 minutes.
2. Preheat the grill to medium heat; Thread the shrimp onto skewers and grill for 2-3 minutes per side, until pink and opaque.
3. Garnish with fresh parsley and serve with a side of vegetables or a salad.

Nutritional Content (per serving)	Storage Tips	Cooking and Ingredients Tips
- Calories: 180 kcal - Total Fat: 9g - Protein: 22g - Carbohydrates: 2g - Sugars: 0g - Fiber: 0g - Sodium: 190mg	Store grilled shrimp in an airtight container in the refrigerator for up to 2 days. Reheat gently on the stovetop or enjoy cold in a salad.	If you don't have a grill, you can cook the shrimp on a stovetop grill pan or bake in the oven. Use wooden skewers soaked in water for 30 minutes to prevent burning on the grill.

TUNA-STUFFED BELL PEPPERS

These bell peppers are stuffed with a mixture of tuna, Greek yogurt, and fresh herbs.

Cooking Details

Prep 10 (Mins)

Time 25 (Mins)

Serves 4

Ingredients

- 4 large bell peppers, halved and seeded
- 2 cans tuna in water, drained (5 oz each)
- 1/4 cup Greek yogurt (low-fat)
- 2 tbsp olive oil
- 1 tbsp Dijon mustard
- 1/2 tsp garlic powder
- 1/4 tsp paprika
- 2 tbsp fresh parsley, chopped
- Salt and pepper to taste

Direction

1. Preheat the oven to 375°F (190°C).
2. In a large bowl, combine tuna, Greek yogurt, olive oil, mustard, garlic powder, paprika, parsley, salt, and pepper.
3. Stuff the bell pepper halves with the tuna mixture and place them in a baking dish.
4. Bake for 25 minutes until the peppers are tender.
5. Serve warm or at room temperature.

Nutritional Content (per serving)	Storage Tips	Cooking and Ingredients Tips
• Calories: 220 kcal • Total Fat: 9g • Protein: 24g • Carbohydrates: 10g • Sugars: 5g • Fiber: 3g • Sodium: 320mg	• Store leftovers in the fridge for up to 3 days. These can be enjoyed cold or gently reheated in the oven.	• For a dairy-free option, replace Greek yogurt with mashed avocado. • You can use any color bell peppers, but red and yellow peppers have a sweeter flavor.

SALMON AND SPINACH FRITTATA

This easy salmon and spinach frittata is rich in omega-3s, vitamin D, and protein. It's a perfect option for seniors looking to start their day with a filling, blood-sugar-friendly breakfast.

Cooking Details

Prep 25 (Mins)

Time 10 (Mins)

Serves 6

Ingredients

- 6 large eggs
- 1/2 cup cooked salmon, flaked
- 1 cup fresh spinach, chopped
- 1/4 cup unsweetened almond milk
- 1/4 cup feta cheese (optional)
- 1 tbsp olive oil
- Salt and pepper to taste
- Fresh parsley, for garnish

Direction

1. Preheat the oven to 350°F (175°C).
2. In a bowl, whisk the eggs, almond milk, salt, and pepper.
3. Heat olive oil in an oven-safe skillet over medium heat. Sauté the spinach for 2 minutes until wilted; Pour the egg mixture into the skillet, then add the flaked salmon and feta cheese.
4. Transfer the skillet to the oven and bake for 20-25 minutes, or until the frittata is set; Garnish with fresh parsley and serve.

Nutritional Content (per serving)	Storage Tips	Cooking and Ingredients Tips
• Calories: 180 kcal • Total Fat: 12g • Protein: 15g • Carbohydrates: 2g • Sugars: 1g • Fiber: 1g • Sodium: 200mg	Store leftovers in the fridge for up to 3 days. This frittata can be enjoyed warm or cold.	You can substitute spinach with kale or arugula for a different flavor profile. Use canned salmon as a convenient alternative to fresh salmon.

Chapter Nine

Beef, Pork, and Lamb

LEAN BEEF AND VEGGIE STIR-FRY

This stir-fry recipe features lean beef and a mix of low-glycemic vegetables, making it a diabetes-friendly meal.

Ingredients

- 1 lb lean beef sirloin, thinly sliced
- 1 tbsp olive oil
- 1 medium red bell pepper, sliced
- 1 medium green bell pepper, sliced
- 1 cup broccoli florets;
- 1 medium onion, sliced
- 2 cloves garlic, minced
- 2 tbsp low-sodium soy sauce
- 1 tbsp fresh ginger, minced
- 1 tbsp rice vinegar; 1 tbsp sesame oil
- 1 tsp black pepper

Direction

1. In a large skillet, heat 1 tbsp of olive oil over medium-high heat. Add the beef strips and cook until browned (about 3-4 minutes). Remove from the skillet and set aside.
2. In the same skillet, add the remaining olive oil, garlic, ginger, broccoli, and bell pepper. Stir-fry for 4-5 minutes until vegetables are tender-crisp.
3. Return the beef to the skillet and add the soy sauce, salt, and pepper. Stir to combine and cook for an additional 2 minutes.
4. Serve hot, garnished with sliced green onions.

Nutritional Content (per serving)	Storage Tips	Cooking and Ingredients Tips
• Calories: 250 kcal • Total Fat: 12g • Protein: 30g • Carbohydrates: 8g • Sugars: 2g • Fiber: 3g • Sodium: 250mg	Store leftovers in an airtight container in the refrigerator for up to 3 days. Reheat in a skillet over medium heat.	Use any vegetables you have on hand, like snap peas or carrots, for variety. For a gluten-free option, replace soy sauce with tamari or coconut aminos.

HERB AND GARLIC ROASTED PORK TENDERLOIN

This flavorful pork tenderloin is roasted with fresh herbs and garlic, creating a succulent main dish that's high in protein and low in carbohydrates.

Ingredients

- 1 lb pork tenderloin
- 2 tbsp olive oil
- 2 tsp dried rosemary
- 2 tsp dried thyme
- 3 garlic cloves, minced
- Salt and pepper to taste

Direction

1. Preheat the oven to 400°F (200°C).
2. Rub the pork tenderloin with olive oil, rosemary, thyme, garlic, salt, and pepper.
3. Place the tenderloin on a baking sheet and roast for 25 minutes, or until the internal temperature reaches 145°F (63°C).
4. Let rest for 5 minutes before slicing. Serve with a side of steamed vegetables.

Nutritional Content (per serving)	Storage Tips	Cooking and Ingredients Tips
• Calories: 210 kcal • Total Fat: 10g • Protein: 30g • Carbohydrates: 1g • Sugars: 0g • Fiber: 0g • Sodium: 90mg	Store in the fridge for up to 4 days. Reheat in the oven or microwave until warmed through.	Fresh herbs can be used instead of dried for more vibrant flavor. Serve with a whole grain like quinoa or brown rice for a balanced meal.

SPICY BEEF TACOS WITH CAULIFLOWER TORTILLAS

These spicy beef tacos are served in low-carb cauliflower tortillas, making them a fun and healthy twist on a classic favorite.

Cooking Details

🍳 Prep 15 (Mins)

🕐 Time 15 (Mins)

🍴 Serves 4

Ingredients

- 1 lb lean ground beef
- 1 tbsp olive oil; 1 small onion, diced
- 2 cloves garlic, minced
- 1 tbsp taco seasoning (low-sodium)
- 1/2 cup water
- 1 medium cauliflower, grated (for tortillas); 1 egg
- Salt and pepper to taste
- Avocado and cilantro, for topping

Direction

1. In a skillet, heat olive oil over medium heat. Add onion and garlic, sauté until soft.
2. Add ground beef, taco seasoning, water, salt, and pepper. Cook until beef is browned and cooked through (about 5-7 minutes)
3. For the tortillas, preheat oven to 400°F (200°C). In a bowl, mix grated cauliflower, egg, salt, and pepper. Form small tortillas on a baking sheet; Bake for 10-12 minutes until golden;
4. Assemble tacos with beef, avocado, and cilantro.

Nutritional Content (per serving)	Storage Tips	Cooking and Ingredients Tips
- Calories: 300 kcal - Total Fat: 16g - Protein: 25g - Carbohydrates: 10g - Sugars: 2g - Fiber: 5g - Sodium: 220mg	- Store cooked beef separately from tortillas in the refrigerator for up to 3 days. Reheat before serving.	- Use any leftover vegetables as toppings for extra flavor and nutrition. - If you prefer a vegetarian option, substitute ground beef with lentils.

LAMB AND SPINACH STUFFED BELL PEPPERS

These lamb and spinach stuffed bell peppers are rich in lean protein and packed with vegetables, making it a healthy and delicious meal. The low-GI ingredients help keep blood sugar levels steady.

Cooking Details

🍳 Prep 20 (Mins)

🕐 Time 30 (Mins)

🍴 Serves 4

Ingredients

- 4 large bell peppers, tops removed and seeds cleaned out
- 1 lb ground lamb
- 1 cup cooked quinoa
- 2 cups spinach, chopped
- 1 small onion, diced
- 1 tsp cumin; 1 tsp paprika
- 1/4 tsp salt; 1/4 tsp black pepper
- 1/2 cup low-sodium tomato sauce

Direction

1. Preheat oven to 375°F (190°C).
2. In a skillet, cook ground lamb until browned. Add onion, spinach, cumin, paprika, salt, and pepper. Cook for 5 minutes.
3. Stir in cooked quinoa. Stuff each bell pepper with the lamb mixture.
4. Pour tomato sauce over each stuffed pepper and place them in a baking dish; Bake for 25-30 minutes until peppers are tender.

Nutritional Content (per serving)	Storage Tips	Cooking and Ingredients Tips
- Calories: 350 kcal - Total Fat: 18g - Protein: 28g - Carbohydrates: 22g - Sugars: 6g - Fiber: 5g - Sodium: 310mg	Refrigerate leftovers for up to 3 days or freeze for 1 month.	Swap lamb with ground turkey for a lighter option. Try using brown rice instead of quinoa for extra fiber.

BEEF AND MUSHROOM LETTUCE WRAP

These low-carb beef and mushroom lettuce wraps are an easy, delicious meal that's perfect for seniors. They offer a high protein, fiber-rich alternative to traditional wraps, helping manage blood sugar levels.

Cooking Details
- Prep 10 (Mins)
- Time 15 (Mins)
- Serves 4

Ingredients

- 1 lb lean ground beef
- 8 large lettuce leaves (Romaine or butter lettuce)
- 1 cup mushrooms, chopped
- 1 small onion, diced
- 2 garlic cloves, minced
- 1 tbsp olive oil and
- 2 tbsp low-sodium soy sauce
- 1 tsp rice vinegar; 1/4 tsp black pepper
- 1/2 tsp sesame oil (optional)
- 1 tbsp sesame seeds (optional)

Direction

1. Heat olive oil in a skillet over medium-high heat. Sauté garlic and onion for 2 minutes until soft.
2. Add ground beef and cook until browned, about 5-7 minutes.
3. Stir in soy sauce, rice vinegar, and pepper. Remove from heat, drizzle with sesame oil (optional), and spoon into lettuce leaves.
4. Top with sesame seeds and serve as wraps.

Nutritional Content (per serving)	Storage Tips	Cooking and Ingredients Tips
• Calories: 270 kcal • Total Fat: 15g • Protein: 24g • Carbohydrates: 9g • Sugars: 3g • Fiber: 3g • Sodium: 370mg	Store the beef mixture separately in the fridge for up to 3 days. Assemble wraps fresh when serving.	Use iceberg lettuce for a crunchier wrap, or switch mushrooms with zucchini for a different texture. Add a little shredded carrot or cucumber for extra flavor and texture.

PORK TENDERLOIN WITH ROASTED BRUSSELS SPROUTS

This roasted pork tenderloin paired with Brussels sprouts offers a nutrient-dense, diabetes-friendly meal with lean protein and fiber.

Cooking Details
- Prep 10 (Mins)
- Time 25 (Mins)
- Serves 4

Ingredients

- 1 lb pork tenderloin
- 2 cups Brussels sprouts, halved
- 1 tbsp olive oil
- 2 garlic cloves, minced
- 1 tsp dried rosemary
- 1/4 tsp salt
- 1/4 tsp black pepper
- 1 tbsp balsamic vinegar

Direction

1. Preheat oven to 400°F (200°C).
2. Rub the pork tenderloin with olive oil, garlic, rosemary, salt, and pepper. Set aside.
3. Toss Brussels sprouts with 1 tbsp olive oil and balsamic vinegar. Spread on a baking sheet.
4. Place the pork tenderloin on a separate baking sheet. Roast both the pork and Brussels sprouts in the oven for 20-25 minutes.
5. Remove from the oven, let the pork rest for 5 minutes, then slice and serve.

Nutritional Content (per serving)	Storage Tips	Cooking and Ingredients Tips
• Calories: 310 kcal • Total Fat: 14g • Protein: 29g • Carbohydrates: 12g • Sugars: 5g • Fiber: 5g • Sodium: 320mg	• Store leftovers in the fridge for up to 3 days. Reheat the pork gently to avoid drying it out.	• You can swap Brussels sprouts with broccoli or green beans for variety. • Use fresh rosemary for a more intense flavor.

LAMB AND SWEET POTATO STEW

This warm and comforting lamb and sweet potato stew provides a balanced mix of protein, healthy carbs, and fiber.

Cooking Details

🧾 Prep 15 (Mins)

🕐 Time 1   (Mins)

🍴 Serves 6

Ingredients

- 1 lb lean lamb shoulder, cubed
- 1 large sweet potato, cubed
- 1 large carrot, chopped
- 1 onion, chopped;
- 2 garlic cloves, minced
- 4 cups low-sodium chicken or vegetable broth; 1 tsp ground cumin
- 1/2 tsp ground cinnamon
- 1 tbsp olive oil; 1/4 tsp salt
- 1/4 tsp black pepper

Direction

1. Heat olive oil in a large pot over medium-high heat. Add lamb and brown on all sides.
2. Add onion, garlic, cumin, and cinnamon. Sauté for 3 minutes until fragrant.
3. Stir in sweet potato, carrot, and broth. Bring to a boil, then reduce heat and simmer for 50-60 minutes until the lamb is tender.
4. Season with salt and pepper. Garnish with parsley and serve.

Nutritional Content (per serving)	Storage Tips	Cooking and Ingredients Tips
<ul><li>Calories: 340 kcal</li><li>Total Fat: 15g</li><li>Protein: 25g</li><li>Carbohydrates: 25g</li><li>Sugars: 7g</li><li>Fiber: 6g</li><li>Sodium: 330mg</li></ul>	• Refrigerate for up to 4 days or freeze for up to 2 months.	• Replace sweet potatoes with butternut squash for a lower-carb option. • Add extra greens like kale or spinach toward the end of cooking for more fiber.

PORK AND CABBAGE SKILLET

This simple pork and cabbage skillet dish is a quick, low-carb meal that's perfect for seniors with diabetes. It's rich in lean protein and fiber, promoting digestive health while keeping blood sugar stable

Cooking Details

🧾 Prep 10 (Mins)

🕐 Time 20 (Mins)

🍴 Serves 4

Ingredients

- 1 lb ground pork (lean)
- 1 small cabbage, shredded
- 1 small onion, diced
- 2 garlic cloves, minced
- 1 tbsp olive oil; 1/4 tsp salt
- 1/4 tsp black pepper;1 tsp smoked paprika
- 1 tbsp apple cider vinegar
- 1/4 cup low-sodium chicken broth

Direction

1. Heat olive oil in a large skillet over medium-high heat. Add ground pork and cook until browned.
2. Add onion, garlic, and smoked paprika, cooking for 2 minutes until fragrant.
3. Stir in the shredded cabbage and chicken broth. Cook for 10-12 minutes, stirring occasionally, until the cabbage is tender.
4. Season with salt, pepper, and apple cider vinegar. Serve hot.

Nutritional Content (per serving)	Storage Tips	Cooking and Ingredients Tips
<ul><li>Calories: 280 kcal</li><li>Total Fat: 16g</li><li>Protein: 23g</li><li>Carbohydrates: 10g</li><li>Sugars: 4g</li><li>Fiber: 4g</li><li>Sodium: 300mg</li></ul>	Store leftovers in the fridge for up to 3 days. Reheat gently in a skillet or microwave.	Swap cabbage with Brussels sprouts or kale for a different texture. Ground turkey or chicken can be used instead of pork for a leaner option.

Chapter Ten

Gluten -Free Meal

PROTEIN-PACKED QUINOA STIR-FRY

This vibrant quinoa stir-fry is packed with fiber and protein, making it a great option for a balanced meal that supports stable blood sugar levels.

Ingredients

- 1 cup quinoa, rinsed
- 2 cups vegetable broth
- 1 tbsp olive oil
- 1 red bell pepper, diced
- 1 zucchini, diced; 1 cup broccoli florets
- 1 cup snap peas
- 2 garlic cloves, minced
- 1 tbsp low-sodium soy sauce
- 1 tsp sesame oil (optional)
- Fresh parsley for garnish

Direction

1. In a saucepan, combine quinoa and vegetable broth. Bring to a boil, then reduce heat and simmer covered for about 15 minutes, or until quinoa is fluffy and liquid is absorbed; In a large skillet, heat olive oil over medium heat. Add garlic and sauté for 1 minute.
2. Add red bell pepper, zucchini, broccoli, and snap peas. Stir-fry for 5-7 minutes until vegetables are tender; Stir in cooked quinoa, soy sauce, and sesame oil. Cook for an additional 2 minutes, mixing well.
3. Garnish with fresh parsley before serving.

Nutritional Content (per serving)	Storage Tips	Cooking and Ingredients Tips
• Calories: 340 kcal • Total Fat: 15g • Protein: 25g • Carbohydrates: 25g • Sugars: 7g • Fiber: 6g • Sodium: 330mg	Store in an airtight container in the fridge for up to 3 days. Reheat in a skillet or microwave.	Feel free to swap in any seasonal vegetables you have on hand, like asparagus or carrots.

CHICKPEA SALAD WITH AVOCADO DRESSING

This refreshing chickpea salad is filled with protein and healthy fats, making it a filling option for lunch or dinner. The avocado dressing adds creaminess without gluten.

Ingredients

- 1 can (15 oz) chickpeas, rinsed and drained
- 1 cucumber, diced
- 1 cup cherry tomatoes, halved
- 1/4 red onion, diced
- 1 bell pepper, diced
- 1 avocado; 2 tbsp lemon juice
- 1 clove garlic; Salt and pepper to taste
- Fresh cilantro for garnish

Direction

1. In a large bowl, combine chickpeas, cucumber, cherry tomatoes, red onion, and bell pepper.
2. In a blender, combine avocado, lemon juice, garlic, salt, and pepper. Blend until smooth and creamy.
3. Pour the avocado dressing over the salad and toss gently to combine.
4. Garnish with fresh cilantro before serving.

Nutritional Content (per serving)	Storage Tips	Cooking and Ingredients Tips
• Calories: 280 kcal • Total Fat: 14g • Protein: 10g • Carbohydrates: 34g • Sugars: 4g • Fiber: 10g • Sodium: 120mg	Store the salad in the fridge for up to 2 days. Keep dressing separate until ready to serve to avoid sogginess.	You can add any other veggies you like, such as shredded carrots or radishes for extra crunch.

ZUCCHINI NOODLES WITH PESTO & CHERRY TOMATOES

This low-carb dish is perfect for seniors looking to enjoy pasta-like flavors without the gluten. The zucchini noodles are light and refreshing, topped with a homemade pesto.

Cooking Details
- Prep 10 (Mins)
- Time 10 (Mins)
- Serves 4

Ingredients

- 4 medium zucchinis, spiralized
- 1 cup cherry tomatoes, halved
- 1/4 cup pesto (store-bought or homemade)
- 1 tbsp olive oil
- Salt and pepper to taste
- Grated Parmesan cheese for garnish (optional)

Direction

1. Heat olive oil in a large skillet over medium heat. Add zucchini noodles and sauté for 3-5 minutes until slightly softened.
2. Stir in cherry tomatoes and cook for another 2 minutes until heated through.
3. Remove from heat, add pesto, and mix well to combine. Season with salt and pepper.
4. Serve immediately, garnished with grated Parmesan cheese if desired.

Nutritional Content (per serving)	Storage Tips	Cooking and Ingredients Tips
• Calories: 180 kcal • Total Fat: 14g • Protein: 4g • Carbohydrates: 10g • Sugars: 4g • Fiber: 3g • Sodium: 200mg	Store leftovers in the fridge for up to 2 days. Reheat gently to avoid overcooking the zucchini.	For homemade pesto, blend basil, garlic, pine nuts, olive oil, and a little lemon juice. Adjust ingredients to taste.

BAKED SWEET POTATO WITH BLACK BEANS AND FETA

This hearty baked sweet potato is filled with protein-rich black beans and topped with creamy feta. It's nutritious and satisfying, making it a great meal choice for any time of the day.

Cooking Details
- Prep 10 (Mins)
- Time 45 (Mins)
- Serves 4

Ingredients

- 4 medium sweet potatoes
- 1 can (15 oz) black beans, rinsed and drained
- 1 cup feta cheese, crumbled
- 1 tsp cumin
- 1 tsp paprika
- Salt and pepper to taste
- Fresh cilantro for garnish (optional)

Direction

1. Pierce sweet potatoes with a fork and bake at 400°F (200°C) for 45-50 minutes until tender.
2. Warm black beans in a skillet with a pinch of cumin and paprika.
3. Slice the baked sweet potatoes open and stuff them with the seasoned black beans.
4. Sprinkle with crumbled feta cheese and garnish with fresh cilantro. Serve warm.

Nutritional Content (per serving)	Storage Tips	Cooking and Ingredients Tips
• Calories: 320 kcal • Total Fat: 12g • Protein: 15g • Carbohydrates: 42g • Sugars: 6g • Fiber: 10g • Sodium: 380mg	Store leftovers in the fridge for up to 3 days. Reheat in the microwave until warmed through.	For added flavor, try adding a squeeze of lime juice over the beans before serving.

LENTIL SOUP WITH SPINACH AND CARROTS

This comforting lentil soup is hearty and nutrient-dense, packed with fiber and protein. Spinach adds a boost of vitamins, making this a great option for seniors.

Cooking Details

Prep 10 (Mins)
Time 30 (Mins)
Serves 4

Ingredients

- 1 cup green or brown lentils, rinsed
- 4 cups low-sodium vegetable broth
- 1 cup carrots, diced
- 1 cup spinach, chopped
- 1 onion, diced
- 2 garlic cloves, minced
- 1 tbsp olive oil
- 1 tsp cumin
- Salt and pepper to taste

Direction

1. In a large pot, heat olive oil over medium heat. Add onion and garlic, and sauté for 2-3 minutes until softened.
2. Add carrots and lentils, and stir for 1-2 minutes. Pour in vegetable broth and bring to a boil.
3. Reduce heat to simmer and cook for about 25 minutes until lentils are tender.
4. Stir in spinach, season with salt, pepper, and cumin. Cook for an additional 5 minutes. Serve hot.

Nutritional Content (per serving)	Storage Tips	Cooking and Ingredients Tips
• Calories: 230 kcal • Total Fat: 5g • Protein: 15g • Carbohydrates: 35g • Sugars: 4g • Fiber: 12g • Sodium: 300mg	Refrigerate leftovers for up to 4 days or freeze for up to 2 months.	Add diced tomatoes or bell peppers for extra flavor and nutrients.

EGG AND VEGETABLE BREAKFAST MUFFINS

These easy-to-make egg muffins are packed with veggies and make for a great on-the-go breakfast or snack option, keeping energy levels steady throughout the day.

Cooking Details

Prep 10 (Mins)
Time 20 (Mins)
Serves 6

Ingredients

- 6 large eggs
- 1 cup spinach, chopped
- 1/2 bell pepper, diced
- 1/2 onion, diced
- 1/2 cup shredded cheese
- Salt and pepper to taste
- Cooking spray or muffin liners

Direction

1. Preheat oven to 350°F (175°C). Lightly grease a muffin tin or use muffin liners; In a bowl, whisk together eggs, salt, and pepper.
2. Add spinach, bell pepper, onion, and cheese (if using) to the egg mixture. Stir to combine.
3. Pour the mixture evenly into the muffin tin, filling each cup about 3/4 full; Bake for 20 minutes or until the eggs are set and lightly browned. Let cool slightly before removing from the tin.

Nutritional Content (per serving)	Storage Tips	Cooking and Ingredients Tips
• Calories: 150 kcal • Total Fat: 10g • Protein: 12g • Carbohydrates: 5g • Sugars: 1g • Fiber: 1g • Sodium: 200mg	Store in an airtight container in the fridge for up to 4 days. Reheat in the microwave.	Feel free to substitute any vegetables you like, such as mushrooms or zucchini.

SALMON WITH QUINOA AND ASPARAGUS

This nutritious dish features baked salmon served over a bed of quinoa and roasted asparagus, providing a balance of protein, healthy fats, and fiber.

Ingredients

- 4 salmon fillets (4-6 oz each)
- 1 cup quinoa, rinsed
- 2 cups vegetable broth
- 1 bunch asparagus, trimmed
- 2 tbsp olive oil
- 1 lemon, sliced
- Salt and pepper to taste
- Fresh dill for garnish (optional)

Direction

1. Preheat oven to 400°F (200°C).
2. In a saucepan, combine quinoa and vegetable broth. Bring to a boil, then reduce heat and simmer for 15 minutes until fluffy.
3. Arrange asparagus on a baking sheet, drizzle with 1 tbsp olive oil, and season with salt and pepper. Place salmon fillets on the same sheet, drizzle with remaining olive oil, and top with lemon slices.
4. Bake for 15-20 minutes until the salmon is cooked through and flakes easily with a fork; Serve.

Nutritional Content (per serving)	Storage Tips	Cooking and Ingredients Tips
• Calories: 400 kcal • Total Fat: 20g • Protein: 30g • Carbohydrates: 30g • Sugars: 2g • Fiber: 6g • Sodium: 220mg	Store leftovers in the fridge for up to 3 days. Reheat gently in the microwave or oven.	Feel free to substitute any vegetables you like, such as mushrooYou can replace salmon with other fatty fish like mackerel or trout for variety.ms or zucchini.

STUFFED BELL PEPPERS WITH QUINOA AND BLACK BEANS

These colorful stuffed bell peppers are filled with a delicious mix of quinoa and black beans, making for a fiber-rich, nutrient-dense meal.

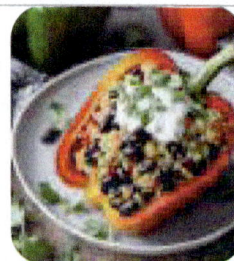

Ingredients

- 4 large bell peppers, halved and seeded
- 1 cup cooked quinoa
- 1 can (15 oz) black beans, rinsed and drained
- 1 cup corn (fresh or frozen)
- 1 tsp cumin; 1 tsp chili powder
- 1/2 cup shredded cheese (optional)
- Salt and pepper to taste

Direction

1. Preheat oven to 375°F (190°C). Place halved bell peppers in a baking dish, cut side up. In a bowl, mix cooked quinoa, black beans, corn, cumin, chili powder, salt, and pepper. Stir well to combine.
2. Stuff each bell pepper half with the quinoa mixture, pressing down gently. If using, sprinkle shredded cheese on top of each stuffed pepper; Cover the dish with foil and bake for 25 minutes. Remove the foil and bake for an additional 5 minutes to melt the cheese (if used).

Nutritional Content (per serving)	Storage Tips	Cooking and Ingredients Tips
• Calories: 290 kcal • Total Fat: 7g • Protein: 13g • Carbohydrates: 44g • Sugars: 4g • Fiber: 10g • Sodium: 280mg	Store leftovers in the fridge for up to 4 days. Reheat in the oven or microwave.	Store leftovers in the fridge for up to 4 days. Reheat in the oven or microwave.

OVEN-BAKED CAULIFLOWER FRITTERS

These crispy cauliflower fritters are a fantastic low-carb alternative to traditional fritters. They are packed with flavor and nutrients, making them a perfect snack or side dish.

Cooking Details

Prep 15 (Mins)

Time 20 (Mins)

Serves 4

Ingredients

- 1 small head of cauliflower, grated
- 1/2 cup almond flour
- 2 large eggs
- 1/4 cup green onions, chopped
- 1/2 tsp garlic powder
- Salt and pepper to taste
- Cooking spray or parchment paper

Direction

1. Preheat oven to 400°F (200°C). Line a baking sheet with parchment paper or spray with cooking spray.
2. In a bowl, mix grated cauliflower, almond flour, eggs, green onions, garlic powder, salt, and pepper until well combined.
3. Scoop tablespoons of the mixture onto the prepared baking sheet, flattening them into fritters.
4. Bake for 20 minutes, flipping halfway through, until golden brown.
5. Serve warm with a dipping sauce or yogurt.

Nutritional Content (per serving)	Storage Tips	Cooking and Ingredients Tips
• Calories: 150 kcal • Total Fat: 9g • Protein: 7g • Carbohydrates: 11g • Sugars: 2g • Fiber: 4g • Sodium: 230mg	Store leftovers in the fridge for up to 3 days. Reheat in the oven for the best texture.	Add herbs like parsley or cilantro for extra flavor.

CHIA SEED PUDDING WITH BERRIES

This creamy chia seed pudding is an easy, nutritious breakfast or snack option that's rich in fiber and omega-3 fatty acids. Top with fresh berries for added antioxidants.

Cooking Details

Prep 10 (Mins)

Time 0 (Mins)

Serves 4

Ingredients

- 1/2 cup chia seeds
- 2 cups almond milk (or other plant-based milk)
- 1 tsp vanilla extract
- 1 tbsp maple syrup (optional)
- 1 cup mixed berries (strawberries, blueberries, raspberries)

Direction

1. In a bowl, mix chia seeds, almond milk, vanilla extract, and maple syrup (if using). Stir well to combine.
2. Let the mixture sit for 5 minutes, then stir again to prevent clumping.
3. Cover and refrigerate for at least 4 hours or overnight until it thickens to a pudding-like consistency.
4. Serve chilled, topped with fresh berries.

Nutritional Content (per serving)	Storage Tips	Cooking and Ingredients Tips
• Calories: 180 kcal • Total Fat: 10g • Protein: 6g • Carbohydrates: 22g • Sugars: 4g • Fiber: 10g • Sodium: 80mg	Store in an airtight container in the fridge for up to 5 days.	Store leftovers in the fridge for up to 4 days. Reheat in the oven or microwave.

Chapter Eleven

Vegan Friendly Meal

QUINOA SALAD WITH CHICKPEAS AND SPINACH

A refreshing and nutritious salad that combines protein-packed quinoa and chickpeas with vibrant spinach and a zesty lemon dressing. This dish is rich in fiber and vitamins.

Cooking Details

Prep 15 (Mins)

Time 15 (Mins)

Serves 4

Ingredients

- 1 cup quinoa, rinsed
- 2 cups vegetable broth
- 1 can (15 oz) chickpeas, rinsed and drained
- 2 cups fresh spinach, chopped
- 1/2 red onion, diced
- 1/2 cup cherry tomatoes, halved
- 1/4 cup olive oil; 2 tbsp lemon juice
- Salt and pepper to taste

Direction

1. In a saucepan, combine quinoa and vegetable broth. Bring to a boil, then reduce heat and simmer for about 15 minutes until liquid is absorbed and quinoa is fluffy.
2. In a large bowl, mix together chickpeas, spinach, red onion, and cherry tomatoes.
3. In a small bowl, whisk together olive oil, lemon juice, salt, and pepper.
4. Add cooked quinoa to the salad bowl and pour the dressing over. Toss gently to combine. Serve chilled or at room temperature.

Nutritional Content (per serving)	Storage Tips	Cooking and Ingredients Tips
• Calories: 290 kcal • Total Fat: 12g • Protein: 10g • Carbohydrates: 39g • Sugars: 3g • Fiber: 8g • Sodium: 130mg	Store in an airtight container in the fridge for up to 3 days. The flavors will enhance as it sits.	Feel free to add other vegetables like bell peppers or cucumbers for extra crunch and nutrients.

LENTIL & VEGETABLE SOUP

This hearty soup is packed with lentils and a variety of vegetables, making it a comforting meal rich in protein and fiber. Perfect for a cozy day.

Cooking Details

Prep 10 (Mins)

Time 30 (Mins)

Serves 4

Ingredients

- 1 cup green or brown lentils, rinsed
- 4 cups low-sodium vegetable broth
- 1 onion, diced; 2 carrots, diced
- 2 celery stalks, diced
- 2 garlic cloves, minced
- 1 can (14 oz) diced tomatoes
- 1 tsp thyme; 1 tsp cumin
- Salt and pepper to taste
- 2 cups kale or spinach, chopped

Direction

1. In a large pot, heat a little water over medium heat. Add onion, garlic, carrots, and celery. Sauté for 5 minutes until vegetables are softened.
2. Add lentils, vegetable broth, diced tomatoes, thyme, cumin, salt, and pepper. Bring to a boil.
3. Reduce heat and simmer for 25 minutes until lentils are tender.
4. Stir in kale or spinach and cook for an additional 5 minutes until wilted. Serve hot.

Nutritional Content (per serving)	Storage Tips	Cooking and Ingredients Tips
• Calories: 220 kcal • Total Fat: 2g • Protein: 12g • Carbohydrates: 38g • Sugars: 4g • Fiber: 15g • Sodium: 300mg	Store in the fridge for up to 5 days or freeze for up to 3 months.	Add spices like paprika or turmeric for added flavor and health benefits.

STUFFED BELL PEPPERS WITH QUINOA & BLACK BEANS

Colorful bell peppers filled with a flavorful mixture of quinoa and black beans make for a satisfying and nutrient-rich meal.

Cooking Details

Prep 15 (Mins)

Time 30 (Mins)

Serves 4

Ingredients

- 4 large bell peppers, halved and seeded
- 1 cup cooked quinoa
- 1 can (15 oz) black beans, rinsed and drained
- 1 cup corn (fresh or frozen)
- 1 tsp cumin; 1 tsp chili powder
- Salt and pepper to taste
- Fresh cilantro for garnish (optional)

Direction

1. Preheat oven to 375°F (190°C). Place halved bell peppers in a baking dish, cut side up.
2. In a bowl, mix cooked quinoa, black beans, corn, cumin, chili powder, salt, and pepper. Stuff each bell pepper half with the quinoa mixture.
3. Cover the dish with foil and bake for 25 minutes. Remove the foil and bake for an additional 5 minutes.
4. Serve garnished with fresh cilantro if desired.

Nutritional Content (per serving)	Storage Tips	Cooking and Ingredients Tips
• Calories: 290 kcal • Total Fat: 7g • Protein: 13g • Carbohydrates: 44g • Sugars: 4g • Fiber: 10g • Sodium: 280mg	Store leftovers in an airtight container in the fridge for up to 4 days.	Experiment with different spices or add diced tomatoes for extra moisture.

CHIA SEED PUDDING WITH ALMOND MILK AND BERRIES

This creamy and nutritious chia seed pudding is an excellent breakfast or snack option, rich in omega-3 fatty acids and antioxidants.

Cooking Details

Prep 10 (Mins)

Time 0 (Mins)

Serves 4

Ingredients

- 1/2 cup chia seeds
- 2 cups unsweetened almond milk
- 1 tsp vanilla extract
- 1 tbsp maple syrup (optional)
- 1 cup mixed berries (fresh or frozen

Direction

1. In a bowl, mix chia seeds, almond milk, vanilla extract, and maple syrup (if using). Stir well to combine.
2. Let the mixture sit for 5 minutes, then stir again to prevent clumping. Cover and refrigerate for at least 4 hours or overnight until it thickens to a pudding-like consistency.
3. Serve chilled, topped with fresh or thawed berries.

Nutritional Content (per serving)	Storage Tips	Cooking and Ingredients Tips
• Calories: 180 kcal • Total Fat: 9g • Protein: 6g • Carbohydrates: 22g • Sugars: 4g • Fiber: 10g • Sodium: 80mg	Store in an airtight container in the fridge for up to 5 days.	Add nuts or seeds for extra crunch and nutrients.

SWEET POTATO AND BLACK BEAN TACOS

These delicious tacos are filled with roasted sweet potatoes and black beans, providing a balanced meal that's satisfying and full of flavor.

Cooking Details

Prep 10 (Mins)

Time 25 (Mins)

Serves 4

Ingredients

- 2 medium sweet potatoes, peeled and diced
- 1 can (15 oz) black beans, rinsed and drained
- 1 tsp cumin; 1 tsp chili powder
- 1 tbsp olive oil
- Salt and pepper to taste
- Corn tortillas (4-8, depending on serving size)
- Fresh avocado and cilantro for topping

Direction

1. Preheat oven to 400°F (200°C). Toss sweet potatoes with olive oil, cumin, chili powder, salt, and pepper. Spread on a baking sheet and roast for 20-25 minutes until tender.
2. In a small saucepan, heat black beans until warmed through.
3. To assemble tacos, warm corn tortillas and fill with roasted sweet potatoes and black beans.
4. Top with sliced avocado and fresh cilantro.

Nutritional Content (per serving)	Storage Tips	Cooking and Ingredients Tips
<ul><li>Calories: 250 kcal</li><li>Total Fat: 8g</li><li>Protein: 9g</li><li>Carbohydrates: 41g</li><li>Sugars: 4g</li><li>Fiber: 12g</li><li>Sodium: 240mg</li></ul>	Store roasted sweet potatoes and black beans separately in the fridge for up to 4 days.	Add lime juice and jalapeños for extra flavor and a spicy kick.

ZUCCHINI NOODLES WITH TOMATO BASIL SAUCE

A light and fresh alternative to traditional pasta, zucchini noodles are topped with a homemade tomato basil sauce, providing a satisfying and low-carb meal.

Cooking Details

Prep 10 (Mins)

Time 15 (Mins)

Serves 4

Ingredients

- 4 medium zucchinis, spiralized
- 2 cups cherry tomatoes, halved
- 1/4 cup fresh basil, chopped
- 2 garlic cloves, minced
- 1 tbsp olive oil
- Salt and pepper to taste
- Nutritional yeast for topping (optional)

Direction

1. In a large skillet, heat olive oil over medium heat. Add garlic and sauté for 1 minute until fragrant.
2. Add cherry tomatoes and cook for 5-7 minutes until softened.
3. Stir in fresh basil, salt, and pepper.
4. In a separate pan, lightly sauté zucchini noodles for 2-3 minutes until just tender. Serve zucchini noodles topped with the tomato basil sauce.

Nutritional Content (per serving)	Storage Tips	Cooking and Ingredients Tips
<ul><li>Calories: 120 kcal</li><li>Total Fat: 5g</li><li>Protein: 4g</li><li>Carbohydrates: 16g</li><li>Sugars: 4g</li><li>Fiber: 5g</li><li>Sodium: 150mg</li></ul>	Store leftover sauce in the fridge for up to 3 days. Noodles are best eaten fresh but can be stored for 1 day.	Add nuts or seeds for extra protein and crunch.

BAKED FALAFEL WITH TAHINI SAUCE

These baked falafel are a healthier twist on the traditional fried version. They're packed with flavor and protein, served with a creamy tahini sauce for dipping.

Cooking Details

- Prep 15 (Mins)
- Time 25 ((Mins)
- Serves 4

Ingredients

- 1 can (15 oz) chickpeas, rinsed and drained
- 1/4 cup fresh parsley, chopped
- 1/4 cup onion, diced
- 2 garlic cloves, minced; 1 tsp cumin
- 1 tsp coriander;
- 1/2 cup whole wheat breadcrumbs
- 2 tbsp olive oil
- Salt and pepper to taste

Direction

1. Preheat oven to 400°F (200°C). Line a baking sheet with parchment paper.
2. In a food processor, combine chickpeas, parsley, onion, garlic, cumin, coriander, breadcrumbs, olive oil, salt, and pepper to blend.
3. Form mixture into small balls and place on the baking sheet. Bake for 20-25 minutes until golden brown.
4. For the tahini sauce, whisk together tahini, lemon juice, minced garlic, and enough water to reach desired consistency. Serve.

Nutritional Content (per serving)	Storage Tips	Cooking and Ingredients Tips
• Calories: 230 kcal • Total Fat: 10g • Protein: 8g • Carbohydrates: 30g • Sugars: 2g • Fiber: 9g • Sodium: 180mg	Store baked falafel in the fridge for up to 4 days. Reheat in the oven for best results.	Add spices like paprika or cayenne for a spicy kick.

OVEN-ROASTED BRUSSELS SPROUTS AND CARROTS

These oven-roasted Brussels sprouts and carrots are a delicious and nutritious side dish, high in fiber and vitamins while being easy to prepare.

Cooking Details

- Prep 10 (Mins)
- Time 25 (Mins)
- Serves 4

Ingredients

- 1 lb Brussels sprouts, halved
- 2 cups carrots, sliced
- 2 tbsp olive oil
- 1 tsp garlic powder
- Salt and pepper to taste
- 1 tbsp balsamic vinegar (optional)

Direction

1. Preheat the oven to 400°F (200°C).
2. Slice Brussels sprouts in half and cut carrots into sticks. Toss with olive oil, salt, pepper, and optional garlic powder.
3. Spread the vegetables on a baking sheet in a single layer and roast for 20-25 minutes, stirring halfway through, until tender and caramelized.
4. Transfer to a serving dish and garnish with fresh parsley or a squeeze of lemon juice if desired.

Nutritional Content (per serving)	Storage Tips	Cooking and Ingredients Tips
• Calories: 150 kcal • Total Fat: 7g • Protein: 3g • Carbohydrates: 22g • Sugars: 5g • Fiber: 6g • Sodium: 150mg	Store leftovers in the fridge for up to 3 days. Reheat in the oven or microwave.	Add spices like rosemary or thyme for enhanced flavor.

OATMEAL WITH ALMOND BUTTER AND BERRIES

A warm and hearty breakfast option, this oatmeal is topped with almond butter and fresh berries, providing a satisfying start to the day.

Ingredients

- 1 cup rolled oats
- 4 cups water or unsweetened almond milk
- 1/4 cup almond butter
- 1 cup mixed berries (fresh or frozen)
- 1 tsp cinnamon
- Sweetener of choice (optional)

Direction

1. In a saucepan, bring water or almond milk to a boil. Add oats and reduce heat to simmer for 5-10 minutes until desired consistency is reached.
2. Stir in cinnamon and sweetener if using.
3. Serve topped with almond butter and berries.

Nutritional Content (per serving)	Storage Tips	Cooking and Ingredients Tips
• Calories: 300 kcal • Total Fat: 12g • Protein: 10g • Carbohydrates: 44g • Sugars: 5g • Fiber: 8g • Sodium: 5mg	Cooked oatmeal can be stored in the fridge for up to 3 days. Reheat with a splash of water or milk.	Swap almond butter for other nut butters or sunflower seed butter for variety.

APPLE CINNAMON OVERNIGHT OATS

A quick and easy breakfast option, these overnight oats are packed with fiber and flavor, making them a nutritious start to the day.

Ingredients

- 1 cup rolled oats
- 2 cups unsweetened almond milk
- 1 apple, diced
- 1 tsp cinnamon
- 1 tbsp chia seeds (optional)
- Sweetener of choice (optional)
- Walnuts for topping (optional)

Direction

1. In a bowl, combine oats, almond milk, diced apple, cinnamon, and chia seeds. Stir well to mix.
2. Cover and refrigerate for at least 4 hours or overnight.
3. Serve cold, topped with walnuts if desired.

Nutritional Content (per serving)	Storage Tips	Cooking and Ingredients Tips
• Calories: 250 kcal • Total Fat: 8g • Protein: 7g • Carbohydrates: 40g • Sugars: 6g • Fiber: 8g • Sodium: 80mg	Store in the fridge for up to 5 days.	Substitute the apple with other fruits like banana or berries for different flavors.

Chapter Twelve

Vegetarian Friendly Meal

QUINOA AND BLACK BEAN SALAD

Light yet satisfying dish. Tossed in a zesty lime dressing, this salad is high in fiber, gluten-free, and perfect for balanced blood sugar management.

Cooking Details

- Prep 15 (Mins)
- Time 15 (mins)
- Serves 4

Ingredients

- 1 cup quinoa
- 2 cups water, 1 bell pepper, diced
- 1 can (15 oz) black beans
- 1/2 cup cherry tomatoes, halved
- 1/4 cup red onion, diced
- 1/4 cup fresh cilantro, chopped
- 1 lime, juiced, 2 tbsp olive oil
- Salt and pepper to taste

Direction

1. In a saucepan, bring water to a boil. Add quinoa, reduce heat to low, cover, and simmer for 15 minutes or until water is absorbed.
2. In a large bowl, combine cooked quinoa, black beans, bell pepper, cherry tomatoes, red onion, and cilantro.
3. In a small bowl, whisk together lime juice, olive oil, salt, and pepper. Pour over the salad and toss to combine.
4. Serve chilled or at room temperature.

Nutritional Content (per serving)	Storage Tips	Cooking and Ingredients Tips
- Calories: 240 kcal - Total Fat: 7g - Protein: 10g - Carbohydrates: 36g - Sugars: 2g - Fiber: 8g - Sodium: 150mg	Store in an airtight container in the fridge for up to 3 days.	Feel free to add other vegetables like cucumbers or corn for extra flavor and crunch.

VEGETABLE LENTIL SOUP

A hearty and nutritious soup packed with lentils and vegetables, providing a comforting meal that supports digestive health and is low in sodium.

Cooking Details

- Prep 10 (Mins)
- Time 30 (Mins)
- Serves 4

Ingredients

- 1 cup green or brown lentils, rinsed
- 4 cups low-sodium vegetable broth
- 1 onion, diced, 2 carrots, diced
- 2 celery stalks, diced,
- 2 garlic cloves, minced
- 1 can (14 oz) diced tomatoes
- 1 tsp dried thyme; 1 tsp cumin
- Salt and pepper to taste

Direction

1. In a large pot, sauté onion, garlic, carrots, and celery over medium heat for 5 minutes until softened.
2. Add lentils, vegetable broth, diced tomatoes, thyme, cumin, salt, and pepper. Bring to a boil.
3. Reduce heat and simmer for 25 minutes until lentils are tender.
4. Serve hot.

Nutritional Content (per serving)	Storage Tips	Cooking and Ingredients Tips
- Calories: 220 kcal - Total Fat: 2g - Protein: 12g - Carbohydrates: 38g - Sugars: 4g - Fiber: 15g - Sodium: 300mg	Store in the fridge for up to 5 days or freeze for up to 3 months.	Add spices like paprika or turmeric for added flavor and health benefits.

STUFFED BELL PEPPERS WITH BROWN RICE & TOFU

Colorful bell peppers filled with a delicious mixture of brown rice and tofu provide a satisfying and nutrient-rich meal that supports balanced blood sugar.

Ingredients

- 4 large bell peppers, halved and seeded
- 1 cup cooked brown rice
- 1 cup firm tofu, crumbled
- 1/2 cup corn (fresh or frozen)
- 1 tsp cumin
- 1 tsp chili powder
- 1/4 cup salsa
- Salt and pepper to taste

Direction

1. Preheat oven to 375°F (190°C). Place halved bell peppers in a baking dish, cut side up.
2. In a bowl, mix cooked brown rice, crumbled tofu, corn, cumin, chili powder, salsa, salt, and pepper.
3. Stuff each bell pepper half with the rice and tofu mixture.
4. Cover the dish with foil and bake for 25 minutes. Remove the foil and bake for an additional 5 minutes.
5. Serve hot.

Nutritional Content (per serving)	Storage Tips	Cooking and Ingredients Tips
• Calories: 260 kcal • Total Fat: 6g • Protein: 12g • Carbohydrates: 44g • Sugars: 4g • Fiber: 10g • Sodium: 280mg	Store leftovers in an airtight container in the fridge for up to 4 days.	Experiment with different spices or add diced tomatoes for extra moisture.

CHICKPEA SALAD WITH AVOCADO AND SPINACH

This vibrant salad combines chickpeas and fresh spinach with creamy avocado, providing a nutrient-dense meal rich in protein and healthy fats.

Ingredients

- 1 can (15 oz) chickpeas, rinsed and drained
- 2 cups fresh spinach, chopped
- 1 avocado, diced
- 1/2 red onion, diced
- 1/4 cup lemon juice
- 2 tbsp olive oil
- Salt and pepper to taste

Direction

1. In a large bowl, combine chickpeas, spinach, avocado, and red onion.
2. In a small bowl, whisk together lemon juice, olive oil, salt, and pepper.
3. Pour the dressing over the salad and toss gently to combine.
4. Serve immediately.

Nutritional Content (per serving)	Storage Tips	Cooking and Ingredients Tips
• Calories: 300 kcal • Total Fat: 16g • Protein: 10g • Carbohydrates: 36g • Sugars: 2g • Fiber: 10g • Sodium: 150mg	Store in an airtight container in the fridge for up to 2 days.	Add other vegetables like cucumbers or bell peppers for added crunch.

BAKED SWEET POTATO FRIES

These delicious sweet potato fries are baked for a healthier twist, providing a tasty side dish that supports blood sugar control with their low glycemic index.

Prep 10 (Mins)
Time 25 (Mins)
Serves 4

Ingredients

- 2 medium sweet potatoes, peeled and cut into fries
- 2 tbsp olive oil
- 1 tsp paprika
- 1/2 tsp garlic powder
- Salt and pepper to taste

Direction

1. Preheat oven to 425°F (220°C). Line a baking sheet with parchment paper.
2. In a bowl, toss sweet potatoes with olive oil, paprika, garlic powder, salt, and pepper.
3. Spread the fries in a single layer on the baking sheet.
4. Bake for 25 minutes, flipping halfway through until crispy and golden.
5. Serve hot.

Nutritional Content (per serving)	Storage Tips	Cooking and Ingredients Tips
- Calories: 180 kcal - Total Fat: 7g - Protein: 2g - Carbohydrates: 28g - Sugars: 6g - Fiber: 4g - Sodium: 120mg	- Store leftovers in an airtight container in the fridge for up to 2 days. Reheat in the oven for best results.	- Experiment with different spices like chili powder or rosemary for added flavor.

ZUCCHINI NOODLES WITH TOMATO BASIL SAUCE

A light and healthy alternative to pasta, zucchini noodles topped with homemade tomato basil sauce create a low-carb meal rich in vitamins and minerals.

Prep 10 (Mins)
Time 15 (Mins)
Serves 4

Ingredients

- 4 medium zucchinis, spiralized
- 2 cups cherry tomatoes, halved
- 1/4 cup fresh basil, chopped
- 2 garlic cloves, minced
- 1 tbsp olive oil
- Salt and pepper to taste
- Nutritional yeast for topping (optional)

Direction

1. In a large skillet, heat olive oil over medium heat. Add garlic and sauté for 1 minute.
2. Add cherry tomatoes and cook for 5-7 minutes until softened.
3. Stir in fresh basil, salt, and pepper.
4. In a separate pan, lightly sauté zucchini noodles for 2-3 minutes until just tender.
5. Serve zucchini noodles topped with tomato basil sauce.

Nutritional Content (per serving)	Storage Tips	Cooking and Ingredients Tips
- Calories: 120 kcal - Total Fat: 5g - Protein: 4g - Carbohydrates: 16g - Sugars: 4g - Fiber: 5g - Sodium: 150mg	- Store leftover sauce in the fridge for up to 3 days. Noodles are best eaten fresh but can be stored for 1 day.	- Add nuts or seeds for extra protein and crunch.

Chapter Thirteen

Sauces, Dips, & Dressings

CREAMY AVOCADO DRESSING

A rich and creamy dressing that adds healthy fats and a fresh taste to salads or as a dip for vegetables. This dressing is easy to make and can elevate any dish.

Cooking Details

Prep 10 (Mins)

Time 0 (mins)

Serves 4

Ingredients

- 1 ripe avocado
- 1/4 cup plain Greek yogurt (or low-fat yogurt)
- 2 tbsp lemon juice
- 1 garlic clove, minced
- Salt and pepper to taste
- Water (to thin if necessary)

Direction

1. In a bowl, scoop out the avocado and add it to a food processor.
2. Add Greek yogurt, lemon juice, minced garlic, salt, and pepper.
3. Blend until smooth, adding water to reach desired consistency.
4. Taste and adjust seasoning if needed.
5. Serve immediately or refrigerate until needed.

Nutritional Content (per serving)	Storage Tips	Cooking and Ingredients Tips
• Calories: 100 kcal • Total Fat: 7g • Protein: 2g • Carbohydrates: 8g • Sugars: 1g • Fiber: 4g • Sodium: 100mg	Store in an airtight container in the fridge for up to 2 days. The dressing may darken; simply stir before serving.	Add fresh herbs like cilantro or basil for additional flavour

ZESTY HUMMUS

This zesty hummus is a great protein-rich dip that pairs well with veggies or whole-grain crackers, offering a flavorful and nutritious snack option.

Cooking Details

Prep 10 (Mins)

Time 0 (Mins)

Serves 6

Ingredients

- 1 can (15 oz) chickpeas, rinsed and drained
- 2 tbsp tahini; 2 tbsp olive oil
- 2 tbsp lemon juice;
- 1 garlic clove, minced
- 1/2 tsp cumin; Water to thin
- Salt and pepper to taste

Direction

1. In a food processor, combine chickpeas, tahini, olive oil, lemon juice, garlic, cumin, salt, and pepper.
2. Blend until smooth, adding water to reach desired consistency.
3. Taste and adjust seasoning if needed.
4. Serve with fresh vegetables or whole-grain crackers.

Nutritional Content (per serving)	Storage Tips	Cooking and Ingredients Tips
• Calories: 120 kcal • Total Fat: 6g • Protein: 5g • Carbohydrates: 14g • Sugars: 1g • Fiber: 4g • Sodium: 200mg	Store in an airtight container in the fridge for up to 5 days.	Experiment with adding roasted red peppers or spinach for different flavors.

TANGY MUSTARD VINAIGRETTE

This tangy mustard vinaigrette adds a delightful kick to salads while providing healthy fats from olive oil and supporting heart health.

Cooking Details
- Prep 5 (Mins)
- Time 0 (mins)
- Serves 4

Ingredients

- 1/4 cup apple cider vinegar
- 1/4 cup olive oil
- 1 tbsp Dijon mustard
- 1 tbsp honey (or sugar substitute)
- Salt and pepper to taste

Direction

1. In a small bowl, whisk together apple cider vinegar, olive oil, Dijon mustard, and honey until well combined.
2. Season with salt and pepper to taste.
3. Serve immediately or refrigerate until ready to use.

Nutritional Content (per serving)	Storage Tips	Cooking and Ingredients Tips
• Calories: 80 kcal • Total Fat: 9g • Protein: 0g • Carbohydrates: 3g • Sugars: 2g • Fiber: 0g • Sodium: 120mg	Store in a sealed jar in the fridge for up to 1 week. Shake well before using.	Try different types of mustard for varied flavors or add herbs like oregano or thyme.

ROASTED RED PEPPER DIP

This roasted red pepper dip is flavorful and colorful, perfect for serving with veggies or whole-grain pita chips. It's a great way to enjoy healthy fats and protein.

Cooking Details
- Prep 10 (Mins)
- Time 20 (Mins)
- Serves 6

Ingredients

- 2 large red bell peppers
- 1 can (15 oz) cannellini beans, rinsed and drained
- 2 tbsp olive oil
- 1 tbsp lemon juice
- 1 garlic clove, minced
- Salt and pepper to taste

Direction

1. Preheat the oven to 425°F (220°C). Place red bell peppers on a baking sheet and roast for 20 minutes until charred, turning occasionally.
2. Once roasted, let them cool, peel off the skin, and remove seeds.
3. In a food processor, combine roasted peppers, cannellini beans, olive oil, lemon juice, garlic, salt, and pepper.
4. Blend until smooth. Serve with veggies or whole-grain pita chips.

Nutritional Content (per serving)	Storage Tips	Cooking and Ingredients Tips
• Calories: 100 kcal • Total Fat: 5g • Protein: 4g • Carbohydrates: 12g • Sugars: 2g • Fiber: 4g • Sodium: 150mg	Store in an airtight container in the fridge for up to 5 days.	For a smoky flavor, add a pinch of smoked paprika.

CREAMY GARLIC YOGURT SAUCE

A creamy garlic yogurt sauce that's perfect for drizzling over salads or as a dip for fresh veggies. It's light, refreshing, and full of flavor.

Cooking Details

Prep 5 (Mins)
Time 0 (mins)
Serves 4

Ingredients

- 1 cup plain Greek yogurt
- 1 garlic clove, minced
- 2 tbsp lemon juice
- 1 tbsp fresh dill or parsley, chopped
- Salt and pepper to taste

Direction

1. In a bowl, combine Greek yogurt, minced garlic, lemon juice, dill, salt, and pepper.
2. Mix until smooth and well combined.
3. Serve immediately or refrigerate until ready to use

Nutritional Content (per serving)	Storage Tips	Cooking and Ingredients Tips
• Calories: 70 kcal • Total Fat: 2g • Protein: 7g • Carbohydrates: 5g • Sugars: 3g • Fiber: 0g • Sodium: 60mg	Store in an airtight container in the fridge for up to 5 days.	Use fresh herbs like cilantro or mint for a different flavor profile.

SWEET AND SPICY SALSA

A vibrant and refreshing salsa that adds flavor to any dish. Packed with vegetables, it's a great way to enjoy the benefits of fresh produce.

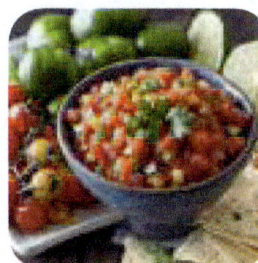

Cooking Details

Prep 10 (Mins)
Time 0 (Mins)
Serves 6

Ingredients

- 2 cups diced tomatoes
- 1/2 cup diced red onion
- 1/4 cup chopped cilantro
- 1 jalapeño, minced (seeds removed for less heat)
- 1 tbsp lime juice
- Salt and pepper to taste

Direction

1. In a bowl, combine diced tomatoes, red onion, cilantro, jalapeño, lime juice, salt, and pepper.
2. Mix well and adjust seasoning if needed.
3. Serve immediately with tortilla chips or as a topping for grilled chicken.

Nutritional Content (per serving)	Storage Tips	Cooking and Ingredients Tips
• Calories: 30 kcal • Total Fat: 0g • Protein: 1g • Carbohydrates: 7g • Sugars: 3g • Fiber: 2g • Sodium: 100mg	Store in an airtight container in the fridge for up to 3 days.	Add diced avocado for creaminess or a pinch of cumin for extra depth.

HERBED YOGURT DRESSING

A versatile herbed yogurt dressing that's perfect for salads or as a dip. It provides a healthy alternative to heavier dressings while adding flavor and creaminess.

Ingredients

- 1 cup plain Greek yogurt
- 2 tbsp apple cider vinegar
- 1 tbsp olive oil
- 1 tsp dried herbs (thyme, oregano, or basil)
- Salt and pepper to taste

Direction

1. In a bowl, whisk together Greek yogurt, apple cider vinegar, olive oil, dried herbs, salt, and pepper.
2. Mix until smooth and well combined.
3. Serve immediately or refrigerate until needed

Nutritional Content (per serving)	Storage Tips	Cooking and Ingredients Tips
• Calories: 70 kcal • Total Fat: 3g • Protein: 7g • Carbohydrates: 4g • Sugars: 2g • Fiber: 0g • Sodium: 60mg	Store in an airtight container in the fridge for up to 5 days.	Fresh herbs can be used instead of dried for enhanced flavor.

LEMON BASIL PESTO

This light and zesty lemon basil pesto is a fresh alternative to traditional pesto. It's great as a pasta dressing, sandwich spread, or a dip for veggies.

Ingredients

- 2 cups fresh basil leaves
- 1/4 cup olive oil
- 2 tbsp lemon juice
- 2 tbsp walnuts (or almonds)
- 1 garlic clove
- Salt and pepper to taste

Direction

1. In a food processor, combine basil leaves, olive oil, lemon juice, walnuts, garlic, salt, and pepper.
2. Blend until smooth, scraping down the sides as necessary.
3. Serve immediately or refrigerate for later use.

Nutritional Content (per serving)	Storage Tips	Cooking and Ingredients Tips
• Calories: 100 kcal • Total Fat: 10g • Protein: 2g • Carbohydrates: 4g • Sugars: 0g • Fiber: 1g • Sodium: 60mg	Store in an airtight container in the fridge for up to 1 week.	Add nutritional yeast for a cheesy flavor without the dairy.

TZATZIKI SAUCE

A refreshing tzatziki sauce made with yogurt and cucumber, perfect for dipping or drizzling over grilled meats and vegetables. It's low in calories and high in flavor.

Cooking Details

Prep 10 (Mins)

Time 0 (mins)

Serves 4

Ingredients

- 1 cup plain Greek yogurt
- 1/2 cucumber, grated and drained
- 1 garlic clove, minced
- 1 tbsp lemon juice
- Salt and pepper to taste
- Fresh dill (optional)

Direction

1. In a bowl, combine Greek yogurt, grated cucumber, minced garlic, lemon juice, salt, and pepper.
2. Mix until well combined. Add dill if desired.
3. Serve immediately or refrigerate until ready to use.

Nutritional Content (per serving)	Storage Tips	Cooking and Ingredients Tips
- Calories: 60 kcal - Total Fat: 2g - Protein: 6g - Carbohydrates: 4g - Sugars: 2g - Fiber: 0g - Sodium: 70mg	Store in an airtight container in the fridge for up to 3 days.	Add a splash of vinegar for an extra tang.

PEANUT BUTTER DRESSING

This creamy peanut butter dressing is perfect for drizzling over salads or as a dip for fresh fruit and vegetables. It's both nutritious and satisfying.

Cooking Details

Prep 5 (Mins)

Time 0 (Mins)

Serves 4

Ingredients

- 1/4 cup natural peanut butter
- 2 tbsp apple cider vinegar
- 1 tbsp honey (or sugar substitute)
- 1/4 cup water (to thin)
- Salt to taste

Direction

1. In a bowl, whisk together peanut butter, apple cider vinegar, honey, and water until smooth.
2. Add more water if a thinner consistency is desired. Season with salt to taste.
3. Serve immediately or refrigerate until ready to use.

Nutritional Content (per serving)	Storage Tips	Cooking and Ingredients Tips
- Calories: 100 kcal - Total Fat: 8g - Protein: 4g - Carbohydrates: 8g - Sugars: 2g - Fiber: 1g - Sodium: 60mg	- Store in an airtight container in the fridge for up to 5 days. Stir before serving.	- Substitute almond butter for a different flavor profile.

Chapter Thirteen

28-Day Meal Plan and Shopping List

Embarking on a new culinary journey can feel overwhelming, especially when managing a busy lifestyle and the desire to make healthier choices. That's why this 28-Day Meal Plan is here—to offer seniors a structured, stress-free approach to balanced eating, specifically designed to stabilize glucose levels and promote overall wellness.

In this chapter, you'll discover a carefully crafted day-by-day meal plan filled with simple, flavorful recipes tailored to meet the unique nutritional needs of seniors. From energizing breakfasts to vibrant lunches and satisfying dinners, each meal is designed to support steady energy, healthy blood sugar levels, and optimal digestion. The recipes are quick and easy to prepare, ensuring they fit seamlessly into your daily routine.

We've removed the guesswork by providing an easy-to-follow structure that simplifies meal planning while keeping you on track with your health goals. To make things even easier, each week comes with a detailed shopping list, so you'll have all the fresh, wholesome ingredients you need at your fingertips—eliminating the need for last-minute store runs or indecision about what to cook.

Whether you're looking to enhance your health, simplify your daily meals, or discover new, enjoyable flavors, this meal plan is your guide. It's designed not only to save you time and effort but also to provide the long-term benefits of a nutrient-rich, diabetes-friendly diet. With this plan, you'll experience the joy of eating delicious, nourishing meals while confidently taking control of your health—one balanced bite at a time.

Week 1 Meal Plan

Day 1
- Breakfast: Quinoa Breakfast Bowl with Berries
- Lunch: Tuna Salad Lettuce Wraps
- Dinner: Grilled Salmon with Asparagus and Quinoa

Day 2
- Breakfast: Oatmeal with Flaxseeds and Almonds
- Lunch: Zucchini Noodles with Pesto and Grilled Chicken
- Dinner: Lentil & Vegetable Soup

Day 3
- Breakfast: Almond Flour Pancakes
- Lunch: Turkey & Avocado Wrap with Spinach
- Dinner: Cauliflower & Chickpea Curry

Day 4
- Breakfast: Cottage Cheese and Tomato Toast
- Lunch: Shrimp and Avocado Salad
- Dinner: Grilled Lemon Garlic Chicken with Steamed Broccoli

Day 5
- Breakfast: Green Smoothie with Avocado and Spinach
- Lunch: Vegetable and Quinoa Stuffed Bell Peppers
- Dinner: Baked Cod with Spinach and Tomatoes

Day 6
- Breakfast: Peanut Butter and Banana Smoothie
- Lunch: Chickpea & Veggie Stir-Fry with Brown Rice
- Dinner: Zucchini Noodles with Pesto and Grilled Shrimp

Day 7
- Breakfast: Savory Chickpea Pancakes with Spinach
- Lunch: Greek Salad with Grilled Chicken
- Dinner: Chicken and Cauliflower Rice Stir-Fry

Shopping List

Produce:
- Avocados (6)
- Bananas (4)
- Berries (strawberries, raspberries, blueberries) (4 cups)
- Spinach (4 cups)
- Mushrooms (1 cup)
- Tomatoes (3)
- Sweet potatoes (4)
- Broccoli (1 head)
- Cauliflower (1 head)
- Asparagus (1 bunch)
- Zucchini (4)
- Bell peppers (4)
- Lemons (2)
- Garlic (3 cloves)
- Onions (2)
- Ginger (1 small piece)
- Carrots (3)
- Mixed salad greens (2 cups)
- Fresh parsley (1 bunch)
- Fresh basil (1 bunch)
- Cucumbers (2)
- Cherry tomatoes (1 cup)

Protein:
- Eggs (18)
- Greek yogurt (2 cups)
- Cottage cheese (1 cup)
- Salmon fillets (4)
- Chicken breasts (4)
- Ground turkey (1 lb)
- Shrimp (12 oz)
- Chickpeas (1 can)
- Lentils (dry or canned) (2 cups)
- Tofu (firm, 1 block)
- Tuna (canned, 2 cans)
- Smoked salmon (6 oz)
- Almond butter (1 jar)
- Peanut butter (1 jar)

Dairy & Dairy Alternatives:
- Coconut milk (1 can)
- Feta cheese (1 cup)

Condiments & Oils:
- Olive oil (1 bottle)
- Coconut oil (1 small jar)
- Vinegar (1 bottle)
- Dijon mustard (1 bottle)
- Tahini (1 jar)

Week 2 Meal Plan	Shopping List

Week 2 Meal Plan

Day 8
- Breakfast: Chia Seed Pudding with Coconut Milk
- Lunch: Grilled Turkey Burgers with Avocado
- Dinner: Salmon & Spinach Salad with Lemon Vinaigrette

Day 9
- Breakfast: Zucchini and Feta Omelette
- Lunch: Turkey and Avocado Lettuce Wraps
- Dinner: Quinoa-Stuffed Bell Peppers

Day 10
- Breakfast: Greek Yogurt Parfait with Nuts and Seeds
- Lunch: Baked Eggplant Parmesan (Low-Carb)
- Dinner: Shrimp and Vegetable Stir-Fry

Day 11
- Breakfast: Spinach and Mushroom Egg Muffins
- Lunch: Lentil & Spinach Stew
- Dinner: Baked Salmon with Asparagus

Day 12
- Breakfast: Avocado Toast with Poached Egg
- Lunch: Roasted Vegetable and Hummus Bowl
- Dinner: Grilled Cod with Tomato Basil Salsa

Day 13
- Breakfast: Almond Flour Pancakes
- Lunch: Sweet Potato & Black Bean Tacos
- Dinner: Turkey Chili

Day 14
- Breakfast: Chia Seed Pudding with Coconut and Pineapple
- Lunch: Minestrone Soup
- Dinner: Baked Chicken with Cauliflower Mash

Shopping List

Produce:
- Avocados (6)
- Bananas (4)
- Berries (4 cups)
- Spinach (4 cups)
- Mushrooms (2 cups)
- Tomatoes (3)
- Sweet potatoes
- Broccoli (1 head)
- Cauliflower (1 head)
- Carrots (4)
- Lemons (2)
- Cucumbers (2)
- Fresh parsley (1 bunch)
- Fresh basil (1 bunch)
- Garlic (3 cloves)
- Onions (2)
- Ginger (1 small piece)
- Mixed salad greens (2 cups)
- Cherry tomatoes (1 cup)

Condiments & Oils:
- Olive oil (1 bottle)
- Coconut oil (1 small jar)
- Dijon mustard (1 bottle)
- Vinegar (1 bottle)
- Tahini (1 jar)

Nuts & Seeds:
- Flaxseeds (1 cup)
- Almonds (1 cup)
- Walnuts (1 cup)
- Chia seeds (1 cup)
- Pumpkin seeds (1 cup)

Grains:
- Oats (1 cup)
- Quinoa (2 cups)
- Brown rice (1 cup)
- Whole grain bread (1 loaf)
- Buckwheat flour (1 bag)
- Almond flour (1 bag)

Protein:
- Eggs (18)
- Greek yogurt (2 cups)
- Cottage cheese (1 cup)
- Chicken breasts (4)
- Ground turkey (1 lb)
- Shrimp (12 oz)
- Lentils (dry or canned) (2 cups)
- Chickpeas (1 can)
- Salmon fillets (4)
- Tuna (canned, 2 cans)

Week 3 Meal Plan

Day 15
- Breakfast: Greek Yogurt Parfait with Walnuts and Strawberries
- Lunch: Baked Tilapia with Lemon
- Dinner: Turkey Meatballs with Tomato Sauce

Day 16
- Breakfast: Peanut Butter and Banana Smoothie
- Lunch: Tuna Salad Stuffed Tomatoes
- Dinner: Lentil Soup with Spinach

Day 17
- Breakfast: Tofu Scramble with Veggies
- Lunch: Chicken and Quinoa Vegetable Soup
- Dinner: Grilled Salmon with Avocado Salsa

Day 18
- Breakfast: Zucchini and Feta Omelette
- Lunch: Roasted Red Pepper and Tomato Soup
- Dinner: Grilled Turkey Skewers with Veggies

Day 19
- Breakfast: Cottage Cheese with Flaxseeds and Blueberries
- Lunch: Chickpea Salad with Avocado Dressing
- Dinner: Shrimp and Zucchini Noodles with Pesto

Day 20
- Breakfast: Egg Muffins with Spinach and Feta
- Lunch: Vegetable Lentil Soup
- Dinner: Grilled Lemon Garlic Shrimp Skewers

Day 21
- Breakfast: Oatmeal with Almond Butter and Berries
- Lunch: Quinoa Salad with Chickpeas and Spinach
- Dinner: Grilled Chicken with Broccoli and Cauliflower Rice

Shopping List

Produce:
- Avocados (6)
- Bananas (4)
- Berries (4 cups)
- Spinach (4 cups)
- Mushrooms (2 cups)
- Tomatoes (4)
- Sweet potatoes (4)
- Zucchini (4)
- Bell peppers (6)
- Broccoli (1 head)
- Cauliflower (1 head)
- Asparagus (1 bunch)
- Garlic (3 cloves)
- Onions (2)
- Lemons (2)
- Cucumbers (2)
- Fresh parsley (1 bunch)
- Fresh basil (1 bunch)
- Carrots (3)
- Ginger (1 small piece)
- Mixed salad greens (2 cups)
- Cherry tomatoes (1 cup)

Grains:
- Oats (1 cup)
- Quinoa (2 cups)
- Brown rice (1 cup)
- Whole grain bread (1 loaf)
- Buckwheat flour (1 bag)
- Almond flour (1 bag)

Condiments & Oils:
- Olive oil (1 bottle)
- Coconut oil (1 small jar)
- Dijon mustard (1 bottle)

Nuts & Seeds:
- Flaxseeds (1 cup)
- Almonds (1 cup)
- Walnuts (1 cup)
- Chia seeds (1 cup)
- Pumpkin seeds (1 cup)

Protein:
- Eggs (18)
- Greek yogurt (2 cups)
- Cottage cheese (1 cup)
- Chicken breasts (4)
- Ground turkey (1 lb)
- Shrimp (12 oz)
- Lentils (dry or canned) (2 cups)
- Chickpeas (1 can)
- Salmon fillets (4)
- Tuna (canned, 2 cans)
- Almond butter (1 jar)
- Peanut butter (1 jar)

Week 4 Meal Plan

Day 22
- Breakfast: Savory Chickpea Pancakes with Spinach
- Lunch: Greek Salad with Grilled Chicken
- Dinner: Baked Salmon with Asparagus

Day 23
- Breakfast: Apple Cinnamon Chia Pudding
- Lunch: Roasted Vegetable and Chickpea Bowl
- Dinner: Stuffed Bell Peppers with Quinoa and Turkey

Day 24
- Breakfast: Smoked Salmon and Avocado Breakfast Wrap
- Lunch: Shrimp and Avocado Salad
- Dinner: Chicken Stir-Fry with Broccoli and Cashews

Day 25
- Breakfast: Egg Muffins with Veggies and Turkey
- Lunch: Creamy Coconut Cauliflower Rice Bowl
- Dinner: Baked Cod with Garlic and Herbs

Day 26
- Breakfast: Greek Yogurt Parfait with Nuts and Berries
- Lunch: Baked Eggplant Parmesan
- Dinner: Grilled Lemon Garlic Chicken with Steamed Broccoli

Day 27
- Breakfast: Cottage Cheese and Cucumber Toast
- Lunch: Chickpea & Veggie Stir-Fry with Brown Rice
- Dinner: Balsamic Chicken with Roasted Brussels Sprouts

Day 28
- Breakfast: Banana Oatmeal Pancakes
- Lunch: Vegetable Stir-Fry with Tofu
- Dinner: Grilled Cod with Tomato Basil Salsa

Shopping List

Produce:
- Avocados (6)
- Bananas (4)
- Berries (4 cups)
- Spinach (4 cups)
- Mushrooms (2 cups)
- Tomatoes (4)
- Sweet potatoes (4)
- Zucchini (4)
- Bell peppers (6)
- Broccoli (1 head)
- Cauliflower (1 head)
- Asparagus (1 bunch)
- Garlic (3 cloves)
- Onions (2)
- Lemons (2)
- Cucumbers (2)
- Fresh parsley (1 bunch)
- Fresh basil (1 bunch)

Grains:
- Oats (1 cup)
- Quinoa (2 cups)
- Brown rice (1 cup)
- Whole grain bread (1 loaf)
- Buckwheat flour (1 bag)
- Almond flour (1 bag)

Nuts & Seeds:
- Flaxseeds (1 cup)
- Almonds (1 cup)
- Walnuts (1 cup)
- Chia seeds (1 cup)
- Pumpkin seeds (1 cup)

Dairy & Dairy Alternatives:
- Coconut milk (1 can)
- Feta cheese (1 cup)

Condiments & Oils:
- Olive oil (1 bottle)
- Coconut oil (1 small jar)
- Dijon mustard
- Vinegar (1 bottle)
- Tahini (1 jar)

Protein:
- Eggs (18)
- Greek yogurt (2 cups)
- Cottage cheese (1 cup)
- Chicken breasts (4)
- Ground turkey (1 lb)
- Shrimp (12 oz)
- Lentils (dry or canned) (2 cups)
- Chickpeas (1 can)
- Salmon fillets (4)
- Tuna (canned, 2 cans)

Conclusion

Congratulations on completing the Glucose Goddess Cookbook for Seniors! By now, you've not only explored over 100 diabetes- and kidney-friendly meals, but you've also taken significant steps toward balancing your blood sugar, restoring your energy, and reclaiming your health. The journey you've embarked on is more than just a temporary change in diet—it's a sustainable lifestyle that supports long-term well-being and vitality.

Throughout this journey, you've discovered that maintaining stable glucose levels doesn't have to be overwhelming or restrictive. With simple, delicious, and easy-to-follow recipes, you've proven that it's possible to manage your health without sacrificing the joy of food. You've also learned that the key to better energy and cutting cravings lies in choosing the right ingredients, focusing on balanced meals, and being mindful of your body's needs.

The beauty of this cookbook is its flexibility. Whether you prefer gluten-free, vegetarian, vegan, or more traditional meals, you've seen how adaptable these recipes can be to suit your preferences. You've experienced the benefits of incorporating high-quality proteins, healthy fats, and fiber-rich foods, all while keeping your meals satisfying and enjoyable. You've also gained confidence in meal planning and preparation, which means you are now well-equipped to continue creating balanced meals that nourish both body and soul.

As you continue on this path, remember that this cookbook is just the beginning. Feel free to explore more variations, experiment with new flavors, and adjust the recipes to fit your evolving needs and tastes. The lessons you've learned here will guide you in making informed, nourishing choices for yourself and your loved ones, ensuring long-lasting health and happiness.

Thank you for trusting this cookbook to support your journey to balanced blood sugar and better health. May the recipes and principles you've embraced continue to inspire you to cook with love, creativity, and purpose for many years to come.

Here's to a healthier, more energized you—one meal at a time!

Appendix 1: The 2024 Dirty Dozen™ and Clean Fifteen™

The Dirty Dozen and the Clean Fifteen™ refer to lists compiled by the Environmental Working Group (EWG), an organization dedicated to environmental health. They analyze data from the USDA and FDA regarding pesticide residues in commercial crops. These lists help consumers make informed choices about buying organic versus conventional produce based on pesticide levels.

The Dirty Dozen includes fruits and vegetables with the highest pesticide loads, while the Clean Fifteen™ comprises produce with lower pesticide residues. It's essential to note that even items on the Clean Fifteen™ may still have pesticide residues, so thorough washing is advised.

Since these lists are updated annually, it's crucial to check the latest version before grocery shopping.
Visit www.ewg.org/FoodNews for the most recent lists and a comprehensive guide to pesticides in produce.

DIRTY DOZEN™	CLEAN FIFTEEN™
◯ Strawberries	◯ Carrots
◯ Spinach	◯ Sweet Potatoes
◯ Kale, collard & mustard greens	◯ Mangoes
◯ Grapes	◯ Mushrooms
◯ Peaches	◯ Watermelon
◯ Pears	◯ Cabbage
◯ Nectarines	◯ Kiwi
◯ Apples	◯ Honeydew melon
◯ Bell & hot Peppers	◯ Asparagus
◯ Cherries	◯ Sweet peas (frozen)
◯ Blueberries	◯ Papaya*
◯ Green Beans	◯ Onions
	◯ Pineapple
	◯ Sweet corn*
	◯ Avocados

Appendix 2: Measurement Conversions

Volume Equivalents (Liquid)

US STANDARD	US STANDARD (OUNCES)	METRIC (APPROXIMATE)
2 tablespoons	1 fl. oz.	30 mL
¼ cup	2 fl. oz.	60 mL
½ cup	4 fl. oz.	120 mL
1 cup	8 fl. oz.	240 mL
1½ cups	12 fl. oz.	355 mL
2 cups or 1 pint	16 fl. oz.	475 mL
4 cups or 1 quart	32 fl. oz.	1 L
1 gallon	128 fl. oz.	4 L

Volume Equivalents (Dry)

US STANDARD	METRIC (APPROXIMATE)
⅛ teaspoon	0.5 mL
¼ teaspoon	1 mL
½ teaspoon	2 mL
¾ teaspoon	4 mL
1 teaspoon	5 mL
1 tablespoon	15 mL
¼ cup	59 mL
⅓ cup	79 mL
½ cup	118 mL
⅔ cup	156 mL
¾ cup	177 mL
1 cup	235 mL
2 cups or 1 pint	475 mL
3 cups	700 mL

Oven Temperatures

FAHRENHEIT	CELSIUS (APPROXIMATE)
250°F	120°C
300°F	150°C
325°F	165°C
350°F	180°C
375°F	190°C
400°F	200°C
425°F	220°C
450°F	230°C

Weight Equivalents

FAHRENHEIT	CELSIUS (APPROXIMATE)
½ ounce	15g
1 ounce	30g
2 ounces	60g
4 ounces	115g
8 ounces	225g
12 ounces	340g
16 ounces or 1 pound	455g

Appendix 3: Recipe Index

S

- Salmon and Spinach Frittata, 54
- Salmon with Quinoa and Asparagus, 64
- Sautéed Shrimp with Garlic and Spinach, 25
- Shrimp and Zucchini Noodles with Pesto, 52
- Spicy Beef Tacos with Cauliflower Tortillas, 57
- Spinach and Mushroom Egg Muffins, 10
- Spinach and Mushroom Frittata, 41
- Split Pea and Ham Soup, 30
- Stuffed Bell Peppers with Brown Rice & Tofu, 74
- Stuffed Bell Peppers with Quinoa & Black Beans, 64, 68
- Sweet and Spicy Salsa, 79
- Sweet Potato and Black Bean Tacos, 69
- Sweet Potato Veggie Breakfast Hash, 11

T

- Tangy Mustard Vinaigrette, 78
- Thai Coconut Chicken Soup (Tom Kha Gai), 31
- Tofu and Vegetable Stir-Fry, 40
- Tuna and White Bean Salad, 52
- Tuna-Stuffed Bell Peppers, 54
- Turkey & Avocado Wrap with Spinach, 16
- Turkey and Spinach Stuffed Bell Peppers, 33
- Turkey and Veggie Stir-Fry, 12
- Turkey and Zucchini Skillet, 21
- Turkey Chili with Black Beans, 36
- Turkey Zucchini Meatballs with Tomato Basil Sauce, 34
- Tzatziki Sauce, 81

V

- Vegetable Lentil Soup, 73

Z

- Zesty Hummus, 77
- Zucchini and Basil Soup, 30
- Zucchini Noodles with Pesto & Cherry Tomatoes, 62
- Zucchini Noodles with Pesto and Grilled Chicken, 16, 24
- Zucchini Noodles with Pesto, 43
- Zucchini Noodles with Tomato Basil Sauce, 69, 75

Printed in Great Britain
by Amazon